THE DISCOVERY OF YELLOWSTONE PARK

THE DISCOVERY OF YELLOWSTONE PARK

Journal of the Washburn Expedition
to the Yellowstone and Firehole Rivers
in the Year 1870

by Nathaniel Pitt Langford

Foreword by Aubrey L. Haines

UNIVERSITY OF NEBRASKA PRESS · LINCOLN

Preface and index copyright © 1972 by the University of Nebraska Press
International Standard Book Number 0–8032–0710–7
Library of Congress Catalog Card Number 78–93106

1-30-23

The text of this edition is reproduced from Nathaniel Pitt Langford's
edition of 1905

Manufactured in the United States of America

CONTENTS

55936

FOREWORD

Five years after the turn of the century a man whose quiet dignity belied his active life began the writing of a manuscript covering an important exploration he had taken part in some thirty-five years earlier. The man was Nathaniel Pitt Langford, one of the band of explorers who made up the Washburn Expedition of 1870 into the fabulous Yellowstone region, and the account he wrote in the modest brick house on the corner of Sherman and Exchange streets in the city of St. Paul, Minnesota, has stood through the years as the principal record of that early visit to the American wonderland.

As first published by Frank Jay Haynes in 1905, this book had two titles. It was called *The Discovery of Yellowstone Park, 1870*, on the front cover, and within, it was titled *Diary of the Washburn Expedition to the Yellowstone and Firehole Rivers in the Year 1870*. However, both titles were inaccurate, for Langford recorded definitive exploration, not discovery, presenting it in a form which is essentially a reminiscent account drawn from diary and other sources. Thus, it now appears better to emphasize the corporate nature of his work by employing the second form, slightly altered, as the subtitle, which is used here as *Journal of the Washburn Expe-*

*dition to the Yellowstone and Firehole Rivers in the Year
1870;* beyond this deliberate casting of the author as the expedition's scribe, the body of this reprinting is a facsimile of the first edition.[1]

It is not intended that this foreword should replace Langford's introduction; rather, the material added here amplifies his work by increasing the biographical information and filling in some chinks. A broader background, particularly in regard to the considerable knowledge of the Yellowstone region and it features prior to the period of definitive exploration, and to the development of the national park idea, is available in present or forthcoming publications.[2]

The relationship of Nathaniel Pitt Langford to the events narrated goes deeper than one might suspect. In addition to being the expedition's effective scribe, he was also its spark plug. The introduction to this book opens in 1862, as Langford, then a sickly twenty-year-old former bank clerk, joins the party of Captain James L. Fisk to the Rocky Mountains in the hope of finding both health and fortune in the gold fields. The one came to him naturally in the salubrious climate of Montana, but the other was largely the gift of his influential brothers-in-law, William R. Marshall, later governor of Minnesota, and James Wicks Taylor. It was the latter's rapport with Salmon P. Chase, secretary of the treasury in the cabinet of President Lincoln, which in 1864 got Langford his appointment as collector of internal revenue for the newly formed

---

1. A second edition, published by Jack Ellis Haynes at St. Paul, Minnesota, in 1923, was rearranged to produce a book of smaller size (5 by 6¾ inches) and more pages. Otherwise, the only essential difference in the first and second editions was in the index provided for the latter.

2. Much of the background of this expedition has been presented, in accordance with present knowledge, in the introduction to *The Valley of the Upper Yellowstone,* by Charles W. Cook, David E. Folsom and William Peterson, which is No. 47 in the American Exploration and Travel Series (Norman: University of Oklahoma Press, 1965).

Territory of Montana; and it was that same influence which nearly got him the governorship in 1869—it would have been his except for the conflict between President Johnson and the Senate. This imbroglio deprived Langford of the position he had held and the one he aspired to, and he was left temporarily without political leverage. It was then he turned to a familial interest in promotion of the northern transcontinental railway route.

That dream of the burgeoning fifties was taking form as the Northern Pacific Railway in 1870, a fruition made possible by financier Jay Cooke's decision to handle the sale of $100,-000,000 worth of railway bonds. The campaign he organized that spring was based partly on the work of lecturers who were to acquaint the public with the country the line was to traverse, thereby creating a speculative interest in "Jay Cooke's banana belt" *and* the railroad bonds. Langford was one of that corps, and after a briefing at the great man's estate, Ogontz, near the city of Philadelphia, he immediately returned to Montana Territory, only stopping long enough at the St. Paul headquarters of the army's Department of Dakota to obtain Major General Winfield S. Hancock's promise of a military escort for an expedition into the Yellowstone region. The organization of that expedition went forward rapidly following Langford's arrival at Helena.

The Washburn Expedition is so called from its leader, Henry Dana Washburn, then the surveyor general of Montana Territory. Having been both a general officer in the Civil War and a distinguished member of Congress, this thirty-eight-year-old Indianan (of Vermont stock) had the advantages of his official position and a prestigious past, and was also of just the right temperament to lead that company, "each of whom counted himself a host; all unusually self sufficient and self reliant, and singularly disposed to individual

judgement, and action."[3] His was a leadership which had no
articles of war for backing, but was, instead, based on reason-
ableness, genuine concern, and a willingness to share every
burden of march and camp—though the frailness of his health,
impaired as it was by a lingering consumption contracted in
the trenches before Vicksburg, would have been excuse enough
for sparing himself. Indeed, he undertook guard duty and
scouting in extra measure and suffered exposure from which
his ravaged constitution was unable to recover. Thus reduced
in vigor, he came down with pneumonia and died on January
26, 1871, at the home of his father-in-law in Clinton, Indiana.
Such was the leader of a group which included other remark-
ably uncommon men.

That cautious businessman Samuel Thomas Hauser would
hardly seem the type to go adventuring in the Yellowstone
wilderness. As a civil engineer turned frontier banker and
entrepreneur (and well on his way to becoming a millionaire),
he was, at that time, vigorously directing his energies toward
getting ahead. A prolonged absence from his business affairs
was no frivolous decision, and since he showed no more than
a cursory interest in the features of Wonderland and provided nothing for the press following the Washburn party's
return to civilization, one is led to conclude that Hauser's
junketing was not motivated by those instincts which usually
send tourists and conservationists into a wilderness. Judging
by his subsequent action in securing control of a railroad
right of way into the area by way of the Yellowstone Valley,
he never lost sight of his own interests.[4] All that remains to

---

3. From an address eulogistic of Henry D. Washburn, delivered by
Cornelius Hedges on Sunday evening, January 29, 1871, at the M. E.
Church, Helena, Montana. A typed copy is in the Hedges Papers (VIII,
No. 13), Montana Historical Society, Helena.

4. His charter became the basis for the Northern Pacific's Park Branch
Line. A statement in *Progressive Men of the State of Montana* (Chicago:
A. W. Bowen & Co. [c. 1902]), p. 202, hints at a closer connection with
the Northern Pacific Railroad by calling Hauser an assistant engineer
of that line, but on what authority remains unclear.

be said of this hard-driving man is that he made his way to
the governorship of the Territory of Montana.

Another member of the party with little obvious reason for
undertaking such an arduous trip was a young lawyer named
Cornelius Hedges. He was not an outdoor type of person,
though he had crossed the plains and grubbed in the placers
for a time; rather, he was a frail and scholarly product of Yale
University—a cultured, sensitive man with money problems
and a flair for journalism. It was the latter characteristic
which proved important, for he employed his facile pen to
popularize the Yellowstone region following the expedition's
return. While Hedges is several times referred to as "judge"
in Langford's account, such a title was not his until 1875,
when he became probate judge of the court at Helena;
that, with his service as superintendent of public instruction
for the Territory of Montana, a term as a state senator, and
work for the state historical society and the Masonic order,
occupied the remaining years of a busy life.

Hedges was not the only journalist with the Washburn
party. Walter Trumbull, the eldest son of Senator Lyman
Trumbull of Illinois, also employed an experienced pen in
the service of the wonder-filled region just visited. Then
twenty-four, this young man—the youngster of the expedition
by a half-dozen years—had already been a midshipman in the
Civil War navy, a world traveler, a reporter for the *New
York Sun* and an officeholder in Montana's territorial government. He had also accompanied his father on an inspection
tour of the completed Union Pacific–Central Pacific line in the
summer of 1869 (including a visit to the Yosemite Valley).
Son Walter undoubtedly shared his father's keen interest in
development of the Northern Pacific Railway but nothing has
yet come to light linking him directly to that concern. However, it is likely that his influence following the expedition's
return went beyond the newspaper and magazine articles he

wrote, for as a special correspondent of the *Helena Daily Herald,* he accompanied William H. Clagett during the latter's successful campaign for the office of delegate to Congress from the Territory of Montana, and that close association undoubtedly provided many opportunities for interesting a future congressman in the Yellowstone region. The conclusion to Trumbull's personal narrative is rather different than one would expect. He went to Zanzibar as assistant consul in 1879 and there contracted the consumption which turned the last dozen years of his life into a unrewarded search for health. When death overtook him on October 25, 1891, at his father's house in Springfield, Illinois, he was only forty-five years old.

For Truman C. Everts, the Yellowstone trip was a between-jobs vacation. He had lost his patronage—his position as the assessor of internal revenue for Montana Territory went to another man when Grant's politicians took up the reins of government—and he had already arranged his return to the East. At fifty-four years of age, Everts was the oldster of the group, a Vermont-bred man who had sailed the Great Lakes as a cabin boy on his father's vessels in his youth and was still quite hardy, though very nearsighted. It was his fate to get thoroughly lost in the Yellowstone wilderness, thereby diverting much of the expedition's efforts into fruitless searching. The thirty-seven days Everts spent alone in the wilderness was an experience he barely survived, and the emotional impact of his story, as it was subsequently published in *Scribner's* magazine, was a factor in creating public awareness of the Yellowstone region. That his trial did Everts no lasting harm, is attested by the fact that he remarried at the age of sixty-five, fathered a son at seventy-five, and did not die until the lad was ten years old.

The best woodsman in all that company, with the possible exception of Lieutenant Doane, was Warren Caleb Gillette. A New York State man from Orleans in Ontario County, he

came of French Huguenot stock and had the instincts of a
trader (sharpened by experience gained through clerking and
merchandising following his schooling at Oberlin College),
so he gravitated naturally into storekeeping and related busi-
nesses on the Montana frontier. With his partner, James
King, he expanded his activity to include mining and freighting, and at the time of the Yellowstone expedition, their
particularly profitable enterprise was the operation of a ten-
mile toll road constructed through Little Prickley Pear Canyon
on the road to Fort Benton. Though a businessman, Gillette
was also of a warm, compassionate nature. When the search
for Truman C. Everts had to be abandoned in order to extri-
cate the main party from the wilderness, he voluntarily remained behind in a last, desperate attempt to find the missing
man. Gillette was later prominent as a rancher and a poli-
tician, but he never married. He died at Helena on September 8, 1912.

A well-run expedition must have a chief of commissary,
and that duty was capably performed by Benjamin F. Stickney,
a rakish young merchant of Helena. He was a farm boy who
left his New York State home at the age of nineteen to seek
work on the trans-Mississippi frontier, finding employment
there as a laborer, bridge carpenter, and teamster before join-
ing the stampede to the Montana gold fields. At the mines,
he combined mining and freighting, and at the time of the
Yellowstone expedition also ran a stationery store in Helena.
Stickney later turned to ranching at Craig, where he managed
a store and a ferry crossing on the Missouri River. He married
in 1873 and raised a family of girls.

One of the most interesting—and misunderstood—members
of the Washburn party is Jacob Ward Smith. He had the
misfortune to excite the animus of journalist Langford, with
the result that he fared poorly when the adventures of the
Washburn party were set down. The trouble was that the

two men were about as different as two could be, and they
irriated each other. Jake Smith was a product of New York
City's St. Catharine Street marketplace, where he learned about
life while working in a butcher stall. He grew up a promoter,
with a penchant for gambling and practical jokes—and merci-
less with stupidities and all stuffed shirts, which seems to have
been his opinion of the sensitive, dignified Langford. Moving
to Virginia City, Nevada, in 1859, Jake established himself as
a butcher but soon shifted his interest to the brokerage business, speculating in silver. He rapidly accumulated a fortune
and gained a place as an assemblyman in Nevada's first legis-
lature, but his fortune faded with the silver boom it was
founded on and he moved to Montana Territory in 1866. His
venture at Helena—a partnership known as the Montana Hide
and Fur Company—had just collapsed in bankruptcy, so that
Jake, too, was enjoying a between-jobs vacation when he went
into the Yellowstone wilderness.

The foregoing should be sufficient to show that Jake was
hardly as "inconsequent" as Langford would have him, nor
was his character as bad as hinted. That he was a gambler by
nature is a fact beyond denial, but the idea that he was a dis-
honest gambler goes unsubstantiated. The expedition's diarists
—Doane, Gillette, Hauser, and Hedges—make no mention of
the episode of the beans, purported to have taken place in the
camp at Tower Fall (see pp. 18–19); however, both Hedges
and Gillette allude to a somewhat similar happening at Fort
Ellis prior to the departure of the expedition. As described
by the latter, Jake was the banker and the denouement
came when Hauser attempted to cash his beans, used in
lieu of poker chips, at the agreed-upon ten cents each, only
to find that the bank lacked the means to pay off. There was
no unlimited draft on the bean bag in that instance.[5]

5. "Diary of Warren Caleb Gillette, August 7, 1870, to September 27,
1870," MS, Montana Historical Society, Helena, p. 8 (entry for August 22).

The real subject of contention between these two was the matter of guard duty. Jake was outspokenly against it after the party reached the Yellowstone mountains, considering it a needless discomfort, which it might well have been. Certainly, Langford was prone to exaggerate the Indian danger, as when they were spied upon by a few of the Crow tribe on the second day. Langford thought there were "one hundred of them watching us from behind a high butte as our pack-train passed up the valley" (p. 9), but Lieutenant Doane passed the incident off with these words: "In the afternoon we met several Indians belonging to the Crow Agency, thirty miles below."[6] Much of Langford's nervousness about Indians and guard duty was a direct result of James Stuart's alarming letter (pp. xxxvii–xxxviii). Having had his camp shot into during the dark hours by Crow Indians in the course of that earlier expedition which was attempting to prospect Crow lands on the lower reaches of the Yellowstone River, Stuart was understandably suspicious of the Crows. Hauser had shared the experience, very nearly losing his life, and thus could be expected to reinforce Stuart's apprehensions and his strong feelings about the necessity of a guard.

On the other hand, Jake Smith was too new in Montana Territory to be very much influenced by those events of 1863, and anyhow, he was of a self-reliant, perhaps even brash, nature and not much given to worrying about tomorrow. Before leaving this subject, it must be noted that Cornelius Hedges, in his personal diary, found no fault with Jake (he frequently teamed up with him on guard duty), and the two travelled back to Helena together from Virginia City, having a splendid time along the way.[7]

---

6. U.S. Congress, Senate, *The Report of Lieut. Gustavus C. Doane upon the So-called Yellowstone Expedition of 1870 to the Secretary of War*, 41st Cong., 3d Sess., Senate Exec. Doc. No. 51. See the entry for the second day, August 23.

7. "Diary of Cornelius Hedges, July 6, 1870, to January 29, 1871," MS, Montana Historical Society, Helena, pp. 43–45.

All this only points up the differences between these men; Langford was dignified, scholarly, imaginative, introspective, and very easily bruised, while Jake was boisterous, carefree, generous, and an absolute realist. In a few words, Jake annoyed Nathaniel and the latter wrote off his tormentor as shiftless. Actually, Jake gave *that* the lie by returning to San Francisco and making his million on the stock exchange before dropping dead of apoplexy on January 23, 1897.

The other important member of the Washburn party was the officer who commanded the military escort, First Lieutenant Gustavus Cheeny Doane. It would take considerable space to detail the career of this frontier-raised man. A love of adventure was the mainspring of his life, and it was that which sent him eastward with the "California Hundred" at the onset of the Civil War. At the close of that struggle, he tried life as a carpetbagger in Mississippi and marriage to a Southern belle, but found neither satisfactory and returned to the military life by taking a commission as a lieutenant in the Second United States Cavalry. In the course of hard campaigning on the Northern Plains, he fought the Piegan, Sioux, and Nez Perce Indians, and later the Apaches of Arizona. Between times, he was in demand to escort such parties as the Washburn Expedition, the official exploring parties which entered the Yellowstone region in 1871, and the secretary of war's own Yellowstone party of 1875. Doane was a large, confident man, a superb horseman and a crack shot. He was idolized by his men and respected by the Indians, and though he dreamed of exploring far places—Africa's Nile River, and the Arctic— he died at the relatively young age of fifty-two, entirely broken down by his years of hard service. His greatest achievement remains his official report of this Yellowstone expedition.

Something should be said also of the soldiers who made up the escort. Sergeant William A. Baker was a typical noncommissioned officer of the "Old Army." He was an Irishman who had enlisted in the Second Dragoons in 1854, earned his stripes in Civil War battles, and remained in the postwar army. He was quiet, efficient, and well liked, and he came to an undeserved end when shot to death in a barracks at Fort Ellis in 1874 during an altercation between two soldiers.

Private Charles Moore, who will be everlastingly remembered as the man who made the first pictorial representations of Yellowstone features, was a Canadian who enlisted in the cavalry in 1868. After a hitch with that arm, he reenlisted in the Battalion of Engineers, where he remained to his retirement as a sergeant in 1891.

Private John Williamson, a sallow-complexioned six-footer from Maryland, is notable only because he was selected, along with Private Moore, to accompany Warren C. Gillette on that desperate search for the lost Mr. Everts. He was probably a rugged, resourceful individual, but he didn't care enough about army life to reenlist.

Private George W. McConnell was an Indiana farm boy who also was satisfied with a single hitch. He served as Lieutenant Doane's orderly on the expedition.

Private William Leipler was a skilled German immigrant (a pianoforte maker) who enlisted in the Twentieth New York Cavalry during the Civil War and was unable to readjust to civilian life afterward. He remained in the army, campaigning in the West until his retirement as a sergeant in 1893.

The Washburn party was completed by two packers—Elwyn Bean and Charles Reynolds—and two Negro cooks known to us only as Nute and Johnny.

A most important result of the Washburn party's exploration of the Yellowstone region was the naming of important features. For the most part, the names they bestowed were well chosen and have stood the test of time; however, there are three which have gone somewhat astray.

While the main party was passing around the difficult

swamps at the point where the Upper Yellowstone River
enters the southeast arm of Yellowstone Lake, Langford and
Lieutenant Doane climbed a high peak overlooking the estuary and the lake. This peak (shown on current maps as Colter
Peak) was called Mount Langford by General Washburn in
appreciation of the helpful information brought back by the
climbers, and a somewhat lower summit to the northeast was
named for the lieutenant. The Hayden Survey transferred
those names to other peaks the following summer, and they
have remained there—eight miles too far to the north—despite
Langford's impression that the error had been corrected
(page 7).

The name given another peak in that general area was
similarly shifted. On the morning of the day before Truman
C. Everts was lost, he and Hedges climbed the peak which is
ieally the northern extremity of Two Ocean Plateau. The
event is noted in Hedges's diary as follows:

> Everts & I went up a high mountain at S. end of Lake &
> on left of trail, called in honor of Everts. Very steep, coarse
> rubble. Came near sliding to bottom. Had a splendid view
> of Lake, found it very much cut up. We got back to camp
> before the train started. Moved out in rear with Langford.[8]

It was that summit which Hedges considered "so fitting a
monument" for the comrade they thought had perished in
the Yellowstone wilderness,[9] but after Everts's rescue near the
northern edge of the present park, General Washburn decided
to put the name on an elevation nearer the place where he
was found. However, the information sent out by the res-
cuers, Jack Baronett and George Pritchett, was misunderstood.
The letter sent from Fort Ellis reported finding Everts "on
the summit of the first big mountain beyond Warm Spring

8. Ibid., p. 30.
9. "Mount Everts," in *Helena Daily Herald*, October 8, 1870.

Creek" (p. 101), but two different streams were so called at
that time—Gardner River, because of the hot water received
from Mammoth Hot Springs, and Tower Creek from the
tepid springs near its mouth. General Washburn assumed the
former was meant, and so placed Everts's name on the great
escarpment overlooking Gardner River on the east. Actually,
the rescue occurred on the edge of Blacktail Deer Creek
Plateau, at the head of Elk Creek.[10]

It must be added that Everts was not pleased with that selection; he prefered yet another peak—the one Captain Barlow
named Mount Sheridan in 1871. His claim to that eminence
as the proper Mount Everts was argued in later correspondence with Dr. F. V. Hayden of the United States Geological
Survey of the Territories, but to no avail.[11]

For those who are primarily interested in Langford's recollection of the conversation around the campfire at Madison
Junction on the evening of September 19, where the national
park idea is sometimes considered to have had its origin, it
must be noted that Hedges's suggestion was neither so novel
nor so impressive as the account indicates (pp. 117–118). He
was not the first to suggest specifically that the Yellowstone
region should be reserved for the public use. Acting Governor
Thomas F. Meagher made such a proposal in 1865—presum-
ably in Hedges's hearing[12]—and David E. Folsom, an explorer
of 1869, advanced a similar thought in his conversation with

10. In a letter to Captain George Anderson, March 28, 1895, Hiram M.
Chittenden states: "By the way I got an interesting item from Barronett
[sic] lately. It was he, you know, who found Everts. I was surprised to
learn that he found him over near the 'Devil's Cut' (or 'Gut') and not
on Mt. Everts at all" (Yellowstone Archives, Letters Received).

11. T. C. Everts to F. V. Hayden, February 14, 1872, National Archives,
Microfilm 623, reel 2, frame 0367 (RG 57, Geological Survey, Correspondence Received).

12. This is covered in a letter written by Father F. X. Kuppens, S.J.,
to an unidentified superior, September 3, 1897, and published in *The
Woodstock Letters* 26, no. 3 (1897). Cornelius Hedges's diary for the
period (October 20–29, 1865) is in the collection of the Montana Historical

General Washburn prior to the departure of the 1870 expedition. Whatever mention there was of the desirability of reservation of the Yellowstone region or its wonders was evidently in the form of a restatement which was not taken seriously enough to find a place in any of the extant diaries; that is, those of Doane, Gillette, Hauser, and Hedges.

But this is not the place to undertake a scholarly review of the national park idea (which had roots in our Anglo-Saxon past and was already well-developed), or the creation of Yellowstone National Park—a far more involved development than it often appears to be. For more information on these, the reader is referred to the work mentioned in note 2 and to earlier publications.[13]

Returning to the author of this book, Langford was appointed federal bank examiner for the territories and Pacific Coast states early in 1872, holding that position until September, 1885. During part of the time—from May 2, 1872, to April 18, 1877—he was also the first superintendent of Yellowstone National Park (a nominal stewardship, since there was no appropriation for the park and his job as a federal bank examiner required his full attention).

Langford married Emma Wheaton, the daughter of a St. Paul physician, on November 1, 1876, but his bride died soon after. Eight years later he married her sister, Clara, and entered the insurance business in St. Paul. In 1897 he assumed the presidency of the Ramsey County Board of Control, handling

Society, and has also been published as "An Account of a Trip to Fort Benton in October, 1865, with Acting Governor Thomas F. Meagher to Treat with the Blackfeet Indians," in *Rocky Mountain Magazine* 1, no. 3 (November 1900): 155–58.

13. Albert Matthews, "The Word Park in the United States," *Publications of the Colonial Society of Massachusetts* 8 (April 1904): 373–99; Louis C. Cramton, *Early History of Yellowstone National Park and Its Relationship to National Park Policy* (Washington, D.C.: Government Printing Office, 1932), passim; Hans Huth, "Yosemite: The Story of an Idea," *Sierra Club Bulletin* 33, no. 3 (March 1948): 47–48.

city and county welfare matters until October 18, 1909, when he died at the age of seventy-nine from injuries received in a fall. His was a noteworthy life—as a pioneer, a Mason, and a scholar, and he was justly called "an able man, a noble character."

AUBREY L. HAINES

Bozeman, Montana

INTRODUCTION

When the rumored discovery in the year 1861 of extensive gold placers on Salmon river was confirmed, the intelligence spread through the states like wild fire. Hundreds of men with dependent families, who had been thrown out of employment by the depressed industrial condition of the country and by the Civil War, and still others actuated by a thirst for gain, utilized their available resources in providing means for an immediate migration to the land of promise. Before midsummer they had started on the long and perilous journey. How little did they know of its exposures! The deserts, destitute of water and grass, the alkaline plains where food and drink were alike affected by the poisonous dust, the roving bands of hostile Indians, the treacherous quicksands of river fords, the danger and difficulty of the mountain passes, the death of their companions, their cattle and their horses, breakage of their vehicles, angry and often violent personal altercations—all these fled in the light of the summer sun, the vernal beauty of the plains and the delightfully pure atmosphere which wooed them day by day farther away from the abode of civilization and the protection of law. The most fortunate of this army of adventurers suffered from some of these fruitful causes of disaster. So certain were they to occur in some form that a successful completion of the journey was simply an escape from death. The story of the Indian murders and cruelties alone, which befell hundreds of these hapless emigrants, would fill volumes. Every mile of the several routes across the continent was marked by the decaying carcasses of oxen and horses, which had perished during the period of this hegira to the gold mines. Three months with mules and four with oxen were necessary to make the journey—a journey now completed in five days from ocean to ocean by the railroad. Some of these expeditions, after entering the unexplored region which afterwards became Montana, were arrested by the information that it would be impossible to cross with wagon teams the several mountain ranges between them and the mines.

In the summer of 1862 a company of 130 persons left St. Paul for the Salmon river mines. This Northern overland expedition was confided to the leadership of Captain James L. Fisk, whose previous frontier experience and unquestionable personal courage admirably fitted him for the command of an expedition which owed so much of its final success, as well as its safety during a hazardous journey through a region occupied by hostile Indians, to the vigilance and discipline of its commanding officer. E. H. Burritt was first assistant, the writer was second assistant and commissary, and Samuel R. Bond was secretary. Among those who were selected for guard duty were David E. Folsom, Patrick Doherty (Baptiste), Robert C. Knox, Patrick Bray, Cornelius Bray, Ard Godfrey, and many other well known pioneers of Montana. We started with ox teams on this journey on the 16th day of June, traveling by the way of Fort Abercrombie, old Fort Union, Milk river and Fort Benton, bridging all the streams not fordable on the entire route. Fort Union and

Fort Benton were not United States military forts, but were the old trading posts of the American Fur Company.

This Northern overland route of over 1,600 miles, lay for most of the distance through a partially explored region, filled with numerous bands of the hostile Sioux Indians. It was the year of the Sioux Indian massacre in Minnesota. After a continuous journey of upwards of eighteen weeks we reached Grasshopper creek near the head of the Missouri on the 23d day of October, with our supply of provisions nearly exhausted, and with cattle sore-footed and too much worn out to continue the journey. There we camped for the winter in the midst of the wilderness, 400 miles from the nearest settlement or postoffice, from which we were separated by a region of mountainous country, rendered nearly impassable in the winter by deep snows, and beset for the entire distance by hostile Indians. Disheartening as the prospect was, we felt that it would not do to give way to discouragement. A few venturesome prospectors from the west side of the Rocky Mountains had found gold in small quantities on the bars bordering the stream, and a few traders had followed in their wake with a limited supply of the bare necessaries of life, risking the dangers of Indian attack by the way to obtain large profits as a rightful reward for their temerity. Flour was worth 75 cents per pound in greenbacks, and prices of other commodities were in like proportion, and the placer unpromising; and many of the unemployed started out, some on foot, and some bestride their worn-out animals, into the bleak mountain wilderness, in search of gold. With the certainty of death in its most horrid form if they fell into the hands of a band of prowling Blackfeet Indians, and the thought uppermost in their minds that they could scarcely escape freezing, surely the hope which sustained this little band of wanderers lacked none of those grand elements which sustained the early settlers of our country in their days of disaster and suffering.   Men who cavil with Providence and attribute to luck or chance or accident the escape from massacre and starvation of a company of destitute men, under circumstances like these, are either wanting in gratitude or have never been overtaken by calamity.   My recollection of those gloomy days is all the more vivid because I was among the indigent ones.

This region was then the rendezvous of the Bannack Indians, and we named the settlement "Bannack," not the Scotch name "Bannock," now often given to it.

Montana was organized as a territory on the 26th day of May, 1864, and I continued to reside in that territory until the year 1876, being engaged chiefly in official business of a character which made it necessary, from time to time, for me to visit all portions of the territory.   It is a beautiful country.   Nature displays her wonders there upon the most magnificent scale.   Lofty ranges of mountains, broad and fertile valleys, streams broken into torrents are the scenery of every-day life.   These are rendered enjoyable by clear skies, pure atmosphere and invigorating climate.

Ever since the first year of my residence there I had frequently heard rumors of the existence of wonderful phenomena in the region where the Yellowstone, Wind, Snake and other large rivers take their rise, and as often had determined to improve the first opportunity to visit and explore it, but had been deterred by the presence of unusual and insurmountable dangers.   It was at that time inhabited only by wild beasts and roving bands of hostile Indians.   An occasional trapper or old mountaineer were the only white persons who had ever seen even those portions of it nearest to civilization, previous to the visit of David E. Folsom and C. W. Cook in the year 1869.   Of these some had seen

JAMES BRIDGER.

one, some another object of interest; but as they were all believed to be romancers their stories were received with great distrust.

The old mountaineers of Montana were generally regarded as great fabricators. I have met with many, but never one who was not fond of practicing upon the credulity of those who listened to the recital of his adventures. James Bridger, the discoverer of Great Salt lake, who had a large experience in wild mountain life, wove so much of romance around his Indian adventures that his narrations were generally received with many grains of allowance by his listeners. Probably no man ever had a more varied and interesting experience during a long period of sojourning on the western plains and in the Rocky Mountains than Bridger, and he did not hesitate, if a favorable occasion offered, to "guy" the unsophisticated. At one time when in camp near "Pumpkin Butte," a well-known landmark near Fort Laramie, rising a thousand feet or more above the surrounding plain, a young attache of the party approached Mr. Bridger, and in a rather patronizing manner said: "Mr. Bridger, they tell me that you have lived a long time on these plains and in the mountains." Mr. Bridger, pointing toward "Pumpkin Butte," replied: "Young man, you see that butte over there! Well, that mountain *was a hole in the ground* when I came here."

Bridger's long sojourn in the Rocky Mountains commenced as early as the year 1820, and in 1832 we find him a resident partner in the Rocky Mountain Fur Company. He frequently spent periods of time varying from three months to two years, so far removed from any settlement or trading post, that neither flour nor bread stuffs in any form could be obtained, the only available substitute for bread being the various roots found in the Rocky Mountain region.

I first became acquainted with Bridger in the year 1866. He was then employed by a wagon road company, of which I was president, to conduct the emigration from the states to Montana, by way of Fort Laramie, the Big Horn river and Emigrant gulch. He told me in Virginia City, Mont., at that time, of the existence of hot spouting springs in the vicinity of the source of the Yellowstone and Madison rivers, and said that he had seen a column of water as large as his body, spout as high as the flag pole in Virginia City, which was about sixty (60) feet high. The more I pondered upon this statement, the more I was impressed with the probability of its truth. If he had told me of the existence of falls one thousand feet high, I should have considered his story an exaggeration of a phenomenon he had really beheld; but I did not think that his imagination was sufficiently fertile to originate the story of the existence of a spouting geyser, unless he had really seen one, and I therefore was inclined to give credence to his statement, and to believe that such a wonder did really exist.

I was the more disposed to credit his statement, because of what I had previously read in the report of Captain John Mullan, made to the war department. From my present examination of that report, which was made Feb. 14, 1863, and a copy of which I still have in my possession, I find that Captain Mullan says:

I learned from the Indians, and afterwards confirmed by my own explorations, the fact of the existence of an infinite number of hot springs at the headwaters of the Missouri, Columbia and Yellowstone rivers, and that hot geysers, similar to those of California, exist at the head of the Yellowstone.

Again he speaks of the isochimenal line (a line of even winter temperature), which he says reaches from Fort Lara-

Very truly Yours
D. E. Folsom

mie to the headwaters of the Yellowstone, at the hot spring and geysers of that stream, and continues thence to the Beaver Head valley, and he adds:

This is as true as it is strange, and shows unerringly that there exists in this zone an atmospheric river of heat, flowing through this region, varying in width from one to one hundred miles, according to the physical face of the country.

As early as the year 1866 I first considered the possibility of organizing an expedition for the purpose of exploring the Upper Yellowstone to its source. The first move which I made looking to this end was in 1867 and the next in 1868; but these efforts ended in nothing more than a general discussion of the subject of an exploration, the most potent factor in the abandonment of the enterprise being the threatened outbreaks of the Indians in Gallatin valley.

The following year (1869) the project was again revived, and plans formed for an expedition; but again the hostility of the Indians prevented the accomplishment of our purpose of exploration. Hon. David E. Folsom was enrolled as one of the members of this expedition, and when it was found that no large party could be organized, Mr. Folsom and his partner, C. W. Cook, and Mr. Peterson (a helper on the Folsom ranch), in the face of the threatened dangers from Indians, visited the Grand Cañon, the falls of the Yellowstone and Yellowstone lake, and then turned in a northwesterly direction, emerging into the Lower Geyser basin, where they found a geyser in action, the water of which, says Mr. Folsom in his record of the expedition, "came rushing up and shot into the air at least eighty feet, causing us to stampede for higher ground."

Mr. Folsom, in speaking of the various efforts made to organize an expedition for exploration of the Yellowstone says:

In 1867, an exploring expedition from Virginia City, Montana Territory, was talked of, but for some unknown reason, probably for the want of a sufficient number to engage in it, it was abandoned. The next year another was planned, which enc 1 like the first—in talk. Early in the summer of 1869 the newspapers throughout the Territory announced that a party of citizens from Helena, Virginia City and Bozeman, accompanied by some of the officers stationed at Fort Ellis, with an escort of soldiers, would leave Bozeman about the fifth of September for the Yellowstone country, with the intention of making a through examination of all the wonders with which the region was said to abound. The party was expected to be limited in numbers and to be composed of some of the most prominent men in the Territory, and the writer felt extremely flattered when his earnest request to have his name added to the list was granted. He joined with two personal friends in getting an outfit, and then waited patiently for the other members of the party to perfect their arrangements. About a month before the day fixed for starting, some of the members began to discover that pressing business engagements would prevent their going. Then came news from Fort Ellis that, owing to some changes made in the disposition of troops stationed in the Territory, the military portion of the party would be unable to join the expedition; and our party, which had now dwindled down to ten or twelve persons, thinking it would be unsafe for so small a number to venture where there was a strong probability of meeting with hostile Indians, also abandoned the undertaking. But the writer and his two friends before mentioned, believing that the dangers to be encountered had been magnified, and trusting by vigilance and good luck to avoid them, resolved to attempt the journey at all hazards.

We provided ourselves with five horses—three of them for the saddle, and the other two for carrying our cooking utensils, ammunition, fishing tackle, blankets and buffalo robes, a pick, and a pan, a shovel, an axe, and provisions necessary for a six weeks' trip. We were all well armed with repeating rifles, Colt's six-shooters and sheath-knives,

C. W. Cook

and had besides a double barreled shotgun for small game. We also had a good field glass, a pocket compass and a thermometer.

Mr. Folsom followed the Yellowstone to the lake and crossed over to the Firehole, which he followed up as far as the Excelsior geyser (not then named), but did not visit the Upper Geyser basin. On his return to Helena he related to a few of his intimate friends many of the incidents of his journey, and Mr. Samuel T. Hauser and I invited him to meet a number of the citizens of Helena at the directors' room of the First National Bank in Helena; but on assembling there were so many present who were unknown to Mr. Folsom that he was unwilling to risk his reputation for veracity, by a full recital, in the presence of strangers, of the wonders he had seen. He said that he did not wish to be regarded as a liar by those who were unacquainted with his reputation. But the accounts which he gave to Hauser Gillette and myself renewed in us our determination to visit that region during the following year. Mr. Folsom, however, sent to the Western Monthly of Chicago a carefully prepared account of his expedition, which that magazine published in July, 1870, after cutting out some of the most interesting portions of the story, thus destroying in some measure the continuity of the narrative. The office of the Western Monthly was destroyed by fire before the copies of the magazine containing Mr. Folsom's article were distributed, and the single copy which Mr. Folsom possessed and which he presented to the Historical Society of Montana met a like fate in the great Helena fire. The copy which I possessed and which I afterwards presented to that Society is doubtless the only original copy now in existence; and, for the purpose of preserving the history of the initial step which eventuated in the creation of the Yellowstone

National Park, I re-published, in the year 1894, 500 copies of Mr. Folsom's narrative, for distribution among those most interested in that exploration.

In the spring of 1870, while in St. Paul, I had an interview with Major General Winfield S. Hancock, during which he showed great interest in the plan of exploration which I outlined to him, and expressed a desire to obtain additional information concerning the Yellowstone country which would be of service to him in the disposition of troops for frontier defense, and he assured me that, unless some unforeseen exigency prevented, he would, when the time arrived, give a favorable response to our application for a military escort, if one were needed. Mr. Hauser also had a conference with General Hancock about the same time, and received from him like assurances.

About the 1st of August, 1870, our plans took definite shape, and some twenty men were enrolled as members of the exploring party. About this time the Crow Indians again "broke loose," and a raid of the Gallatin and Yellowstone valleys was threatened, and a majority of those who had enrolled their names, experiencing that decline of courage so aptly illustrated by Bob Acres, suddenly found excuse for withdrawal in various emergent occupations.

After a few days of suspense and doubt, Samuel T. Hauser told me that if he could find two men whom he knew, who would accompany him, he would attempt the journey; and he asked me to join him in a letter to James Stuart, living at Deer Lodge, proposing that he should go with us. Benjamin Stickney, one of the most enthusiastic of our number, also wrote to Mr. Stuart that there were eight persons who would go at all hazards and asked him (Stuart) to be a member of the party. Stuart replied to Hauser and myself as follows:

                    Deer Lodge City, M. T., Aug. 9th, 1870.
Dear Sam and Langford:
  Stickney wrote me that the Yellow Stone party had
dwindled down to eight persons. That is not enough to
stand guard, and I won't go into that country without having a guard every night. From present news it is probable
that the Crows will be scattered on all the headwaters of
the Yellow Stone, and if that is the case, they would not
want any better fun than to clean up a party of eight (that
does not stand guard) and say that the Sioux did it, as they
said when they went through us on the Big Horn. It will
not be safe to go into that country with less than fifteen
men, and not very safe with that number. I would like it
better if it was fight from the start; we would then kill
every Crow that we saw, and take the chances of their
rubbing us out. As it is, we will have to let them alone
until they will get the best of us by stealing our horses or
killing some of us; then we will be so crippled that we
can't do them any damage.
  At the commencement of this letter I said I would not
go unless the party stood guard. I will take that back, for
I am just d——d fool enough to go anywhere that anybody
else is willing to go, only I want it understood that very
likely some of us will lose our hair. I will be on hand Sunday evening, unless I hear that the trip is postponed.
                         Fraternally yours,
                              JAS. STUART.
  Since writing the above, I have received a telegram saying, "twelve of us going certain." Glad to hear it—the
more the better. Will bring two pack horses and one pack
saddle.

  I have preserved this letter of James Stuart for the thirty-
five years since it was received. It was written with a
lead pencil on both sides of a sheet of paper, and I insert
here a photograph of a half-tone reproduction of it. It has
become somewhat illegible and obscure from repeated fold-
ing and unfolding.

Deer Lodge City M. T. Aug 9th 1870

Dear Sam'l Langford:—

Stickney wrote me that the Yellow
Stone party had dwindled down to eight persons
that is not enough to stand guard and I wont
go into that country without having a guard
every night.— From present news it is probable
that all the Crows will be scattered on all the
head waters of the Yellow Stone & if that is
the case they would not want any better fun
than to clean up a party of eight (that does not
stand guard) and say that the Sioux did it
as they said when they went through us on the
Big Horn. It will not be safe to go into that
country with less than fifteen men, and not
very safe with that number.— I would like it
better if it was fight from the start; we would
then kill every Crow that we saw & take the
chances of their cutting us out. As it is, we
will have to let them alone until they will
get the best of us by stealing our horses or
killing some of us: then we will be so crippled

Mr. Stuart was a man of large experience in such enter-
prises as that in which we were about to engage, and was
familiar with all the tricks of Indian craft and sagacity;
and our subsequent experience in meeting the Indians on
the second day of our journey after leaving Fort Ellis, and
their evident hostile intentions, justified in the fullest degree Stuart's apprehensions.

About this time Gen. Henry D. Washburn, the surveyor
general of Montana, joined with Mr. Hauser in a telegram
to General Hancock, at St. Paul, requesting him to provide
the promised escort of a company of cavalry. General Hancock immediately responded, and on August 14th tele-
graphed an order on the commandant at Fort Ellis, near

Bozeman, for such escort as would be deemed necessary to insure the safety of our party.

Just at this critical time I received a letter from Stuart announcing that he had been drawn as a juryman to serve at the term of court then about to open, and that as the federal judge declined to excuse him, he would not be able to join our party. This was a sore and discouraging disappointment both to Hauser and myself, for we felt that in case we had trouble with the Indians Stuart's services to the party would be worth those of half a dozen ordinary men.

A new roster was made up, and I question if there was ever a body of men organized for an exploring expedition, more intelligent or more keenly alive to the risks to be encountered than those then enrolled; and it seems proper that I here speak more specifically of them.

Gen. Henry D. Washburn was the surveyor general of Montana and had been brevetted a major general for services in the Civil War, and had served two terms in the Congress of the United States. Judge Cornelius Hedges was a distinguished and highly esteemed member of the Montana bar. Samuel T. Hauser was a civil engineer, and was president of the First National Bank of Helena. He was afterwards appointed governor of Montana by Grover Cleveland. Warren C. Gillette and Benjamin Stickney were pioneer merchants in Montana. Walter Trumbull was assistant assessor of internal revenue, and a son of United States Senator Lyman Trumbull of Illinois. Truman C. Everts was assessor of internal revenue for Montana, and Nathaniel P. Langford (the writer) had been for nearly five years the United States collector of internal revenue for Montana, and had been appointed governor of Montana by Andrew Johnson, but, owing to the imbroglio of the Senate with Johnson, his appointment was not confirmed.

While we were disappointed in our expectation of having James Stuart for our commander and adviser, General Washburn was chosen captain of the party, and Mr. Stickney was appointed commissary and instructed to put up in proper form a supply of provisions sufficient for thirty (30) days, though we had contemplated a limit of twenty-five (25) days for our absence. Each man promptly paid to Mr. Stickney his share of the estimated expense. When all these preparations had been made, Jake Smith requested permission to be enrolled as a member of our company. Jake was constitutionally unfitted to be a member of such a party of exploration, where vigilance and alertness were essential to safety and success. He was too inconsequent and easy going to command our confidence or to be of much assistance. He seemed to think that his good-natured nonsense would always be a passport to favor and be accepted in the stead of real service, and in my association with him I was frequently reminded of the youth who announced in a newspaper advertisement that he was a poor but pious young man, who desired board in a family where there were small children, and where his Christian example would be considered a sufficient compensation. Jake did not share the view of the other members of our company, that in standing guard, the sentry should resist his inclination to slumber. Mr. Hedges, in his diary, published in Volume V. of the Montana Historical Society publications, on September 13th, thus records an instance of insubordination in standing guard:

Jake made a fuss about his turn, and Washburn stood in his place.

Now that this and like incidents of our journey are in the dim past, let us inscribe for his epitaph what was his own

adopted motto while doing guard duty when menaced by the
Indians on the Yellowstone:

"REQUIESCAT IN PACE."

Of our number, five—General Washburn, Walter Trumbull, Truman C. Everts, Jacob Smith and Lieutenant Doane
—have died. The five members now surviving are Cornelius
Hedges, Samuel T. Hauser, Warren C. Gillette, Benjamin
Stickney and myself.

I have not been able to ascertain the date of death of
either Walter Trumbull or Jacob Smith. Lieutenant Doane
died at Bozeman, Montana, May 5, 1892. His report to the
War Department of our exploration is a classic. Major
Chittenden says:

His fine descriptions have never been surpassed by any
subsequent writer. Although suffering intense physical torture during the greater portion of the trip, it did not extinguish in him the truly poetic ardor with which those
strange phenomena seem to have inspired him.

Dr. Hayden, who first visited this region the year following that of our exploration, says of Lieutenant Doane's
report:

I venture to state as my opinion, that for graphic description and thrilling interest, it has not been surpassed
by any official report made to our government since the
times of Lewis and Clark.

Mr. Everts died at Hyattsville, Md., on the 16th day of
February, 1901, at the age of eighty-five, survived by his
daughter, Elizabeth Everts Verrill, and a young widow, and
also a son nine years old, born when Everts was seventy-six
years of age,—a living monument to bear testimony to
that physical vigor and vitality which carried him through
the "Thirty-seven days of peril," when he was lost from

our party in the dense forest on the southwest shore of Yellowstone lake.

General Washburn died on January 26, 1871, his death being doubtless hastened by the hardships and exposures of our journey, from which many of our party suffered in greater or less degree.

In an eloquent eulogistic address delivered in Helena January 29, 1871, Judge Cornelius Hedges said concerning the naming of Mount Washburn:

On the west bank of the Yellowstone, between Tower Fall and Hell-broth springs, opposite the profoundest chasm of that marvelous river cañon, a mighty sentinel overlooking that region of wonders, rises in its serene and solitary grandeur,—Mount Washburn,—pointing the way his enfranchised spirit was so soon to soar. He was the first to climb its bare, bald summit, and thence reported to us the welcome news that he saw the beautiful lake that had been the proposed object of our journey. By unanimous voice, unsolicited by him, we gave the mountain a name that through coming years shall bear onward the memory of our gallant, generous leader. How little we then thought that he would be the first to live only in memory. * * * The deep forests of evergreen pine that embosom that lake shall typify the ever green spot in our memory where shall cluster the pleasant recollections of our varied experiences on that expedition.

The question is frequently asked, "Who originated the plan of setting apart this region as a National Park?" I answer that Judge Cornelius Hedges of Helena wrote the first articles ever published by the press urging the dedication of this region as a park. The Helena Herald of Nov. 9, 1870, contains a letter of Mr. Hedges, in which he advocated the scheme, and in my lectures delivered in Washington and New York in January, 1871, I directed attention to Mr. Hedges' suggestion, and urged the passage by Congress

of an act setting apart that region as a public park. All
this was several months prior to the first exploration by the
U. S. Geological Survey, in charge of Dr. Hayden. The suggestion that the region should be made into a National Park
was first broached to the members of our party on September 19, 1870, by Mr. Hedges, while we were in camp at
the confluence of the Firehole and Gibbon rivers, as is related in this diary. After the return home of our party, I
was informed by General Washburn that on the eve of the
departure of our expedition from Helena, David E. Folsom
had suggested to him the desirability of creating a park
at the grand cañon and falls of the Yellowstone. This fact
was unknown to Mr. Hedges,—and the boundary lines of
the proposed park were extended by him so as to be com-
mensurate with the wider range of our explorations.

The bill for the creation of the park was introduced in the
House of Representatives by Hon. William H. Clagett, dele-
gate from Montana Territory. On July 9, 1894, William
R. Marshall, Secretary of the Minnesota Historical Society,
wrote to Mr. Clagett, asking him the question: "Who are
entitled to the principal credit for the passage of the act of
Congress establishing the Yellowstone National Park?" Mr.
Clagett replied as follows:

Coeur d'Alene, Idaho, July 14th, 1894.
Wm. R. Marshall,
Secretary Minnesota Historical Society, St. Paul, Minn.
Dear Sir: Your favor of July 9th is just received. I
am glad that you have called my attention to the question, "Who are entitled to the principal credit for the passage of the act of Congress establishing the Yellowstone
National Park?" The history of that measure, as far as
known to me, is as follows, to-wit: In the fall of 1870,
soon after the return of the Washburn-Langford party,
two printers at Deer Lodge City, Montana, went into the
Firehole basin and cut a large number of poles, intending

to come back the next summer and fence in the tract of land containing the principal geysers, and hold posses- sion for speculative purposes, as the Hutchins family so long held the Yosemite valley. One of these men was named Harry Norton. He subsequently wrote a book on the park. The other one was named Brown. He now lives in Spokane, Wash., and both of them in the summer of 1871 worked in the New Northwest office at Deer Lodge. When I learned from them in the late fall of 1870 or spring of 1871 what they intended to do, I remonstrated with them and stated that from the description given by them and by members of Mr. Langford's party, the whole region should be made into a National Park and no pri- vate proprietorship be allowed.

I was elected Delegate to Congress from Montana in August, 1871, and after the election, Nathaniel P. Lang- ford, Cornelius Hedges and myself had a consultation in Helena, and agreed that every effort should be made to establish the Park as soon as possible, and before any per- son had got a serious foothold—Mr. McCartney, at the Mammoth Hot Springs, being the only one who at that time had any improvements made. In December, 1871, Mr. Lang- ford came to Washington and remained there for some time, and we two counseled together about the Park proj- ect. I drew the bill to establish the Park, and never knew Professor Hayden in connection with that bill, except that I requested Mr. Langford to get from him a description of the boundaries of the proposed Park. There was some delay in getting the description, and my recollection is that Langford brought me the description after consulta- tion with Professor Hayden. I then filled the blank in the bill with the description, and the bill passed both Houses of Congress just as it was drawn and without any change or amendment whatsoever.

After the bill was drawn, Langford stated to me that Senator Pomeroy of Kansas was very anxious to have the honor of introducing the bill in the Senate; and as he (Pomeroy) was the chairman of the Senate committee on Public Lands, in order to facilitate its passage, I had a clean copy made of the bill and on the first call day in the

House, introduced the original there, and then went over
to the Senate Chamber and handed the copy to Senator
Pomeroy, who immediately introduced it in the Senate.
The bill passed the Senate first and came to the House,
and passed the House without amendment, at a time when
I happened to be at the other end of the Capitol, and hence
I was not present when it actually passed the House.

Since the passage of this bill there have been so many
men who have claimed the exclusive credit for its passage, that I have lived for twenty years, suffering from a
chronic feeling of disgust whenever the subject was mentioned. So far as my personal knowledge goes, the first
idea of making it a public park occurred to myself; but
from information received from Langford and others, it
has always been my opinion that Hedges, Langford, and
myself formed the same idea about the same time, and
we all three acted together in Montana, and afterwards
Langford and I acted with Professor Hayden in Washington, in the winter of 1871-2.

The fact is that the matter was well under way before
Professor Hayden was ever heard of in connection with
that measure. When he returned to Washington in 1871,
he brought with him a large number of specimens from
different parts of the Park, which were on exhibition in
one of the rooms of the Capitol or in the Smithsonian In-
stitute (one or the other), while Congress was in session,
and he rendered valuable services in exhibiting these specimens and explaining the geological and other features of
the proposed Park, and between him, Langford and myself, I believe there was not a single member of Congress
in either House who was not fully posted by one or the
other of us in personal interviews; so much so, that the
bill practically passed both Houses without objection.

It has always been a pleasure to me to give to Professor
Hayden and to Senator Pomeroy, and Mr. Dawes of Mass.
all of the credit which they deserve in connection with
the passage of that measure, but the truth of the matter
is that the origin of the movement which created the Park
was with Hedges, Langford and myself; and after Con-

gress met, Langford and I probably did two-thirds, if not three-fourths of all the work connected with its passage.

I think that the foregoing letter contains a full statement of what you wish, and I hope that you will be able to correct, at least to some extent, the misconceptions which the selfish vanity of some people has occasioned on the subject.   Very truly yours,

Wm H. Clagett,

It is true that Professor Hayden joined with Mr. Clagett and myself in working for the passage of the act of dedication, but no person can divide with Cornelius Hedges and David E. Folsom the honor of *originating the idea* of creating the Yellowstone Park.

By direction of Major Hiram M. Chittenden there has been erected at the junction of the Firehole and Gibbon rivers a large slab upon which is inscribed the following legend:

JUNCTION

OF THE

GIBBON AND FIREHOLE RIVERS,
FORMING THE MADISON FORK OF THE MISSOURI.

———

ON THE POINT OF LAND BETWEEN THE TRIBUTARY STREAMS, SEPTEMBER 19, 1870, THE CELEBRATED WASHBURN EXPEDITION, WHICH FIRST MADE KNOWN TO THE WORLD THE WONDERS OF THE YELLOWSTONE, WAS ENCAMPED, AND HERE WAS FIRST SUGGESTED THE IDEA OF SETTING APART THIS REGION AS A NATIONAL PARK.

On the south bank of the Madison, just below the junction of these two streams, and overlooking this memorable camping ground, is a lofty escarpment to which has ap-

propriately been given the name "National Park mountain."

I take occasion here to refer to my personal connection
with the Park. Upon the passage by Congress, on March
1, 1872, of the act of dedication, I was appointed superintendent of the Park. I discharged the duties of the office
for more than five years, without compensation of any kind,
and paying my own expenses. Soon after the creation of
the Park the Secretary of the Interior received many applications for leases to run for a long term of years, of tracts
of land in the vicinity of the principal marvels of that region, such as the Grand Cañon and Falls, the Upper Geyser
basin, etc. These applications were invariably referred to
me by the Assistant Secretary of the Interior, Hon. B. R.
Cowen. It was apparent from an examination of these applications that the purpose of the applicants was to enclose
with fences their holdings, and charge visitors an admission
fee. To have permitted this would have defeated the purpose of the act of dedication. In many instances the applicants made earnest pleas, both personally and through their
members in Congress, to the Interior Department and to
myself for an approval of their applications, offering to
speedily make improvements of a value ranging from $100,-
000 to $500,000. I invariably reported unfavorably upon
these alluring propositions, and in no instance was my rec-
ommendation overruled by Secretary Cowen, to whom Secretary Delano had given the charge of the whole matter,
and to Judge Cowen's firmness in resisting the political and
other influences that were brought to bear is largely due the
fact that these early applications for concessions were not
granted. A time should never come when the American
people will have forgotten the services, a generation ago,
of Judge Cowen, in resisting the designs of unscrupulous
men in their efforts to secure possession of the most impor-

tant localities in the Park, nor the later services of George Bird Grinnell, William Hallett Phillips and U. S. Senator George Graham Vest, in the preservation of the wild game of the Park and of the Park itself from the more determined encroachments of private greed.

The second year of my services as superintendent, some of my friends in Congress proposed to give me a salary sufficiently large to pay actual expenses. I requested them to make no effort in this behalf, saying that I feared that some successful applicant for such a salaried position, giving little thought to the matter, would approve the applications for leases; and that as long as I could prevent the granting of any exclusive concessions I would be willing to serve as superintendent without compensation.

Apropos of my official connection with the Park a third of a century ago, is the following letter to me, written by George Bird Grinnell. This personal tribute from one who himself has done so much in behalf of the Park was very gratifying to me.

New York, April 29th, 1903.

Mr. N. P. Langford St. Paul, Minn.,

Dear Sir: I am glad to read the newspaper cutting from the Pioneer Press of April 19th, which you so kindly sent me.

In these days of hurry and bustle, when events of importance crowd so fast on each other that the memory of each is necessarily short lived, it is gratifying to be reminded from time to time of important services rendered to the nation in a past which, though really recent, seems to the younger generation far away.

The service which you performed for the United States, and indeed for the world, in describing the Yellowstone Park, and in setting on foot and persistently advocating the plan to make it a national pleasure ground, will always be remembered; and it is well that public acknowledgment should be made of it occasionally, so that the men of this generation may not forget what they owe to those of the past.

Yours very truly,

GEO. BIRD GRINNELL.

The Act of Congress creating the Park provided that this region should be "set apart for a public park or pleasuring ground for the benefit and enjoyment of the people," but this end has not been accomplished except as the result of untiring vigilance and labor on the part of a very few persons who have never wavered in their loyalty to the Park. It may never be known how nearly the purposes of the Act of Dedication have escaped defeat; but a letter written to me by George Bird Grinnell and an editorial from *Forest and Stream* may reveal to visitors who now enjoy without let or hindrance the wonders of that region, how narrowly this "Temple of the living God," as it has been termed, has escaped desecration at the hands of avaricious money-getters, and becoming a "Den of Thieves."

New York, July 25, 1905.

Mr. N. P. Langford.

Dear Sir: I am very glad that your diary is to be published. It is something that I have long hoped that we might see.

It is true, as you say, that I have for a good many years done what I could toward protecting the game in the Yellowstone Park; but what seems to me more important than that is that *Forest and Stream* for a dozen years carried on, almost single handed, a fight for the integrity of the National Park. If you remember, all through from 1881 or thereabouts to 1890 continued efforts were being made to gain control of the park by one syndicate and another, or to run a railroad through it, or to put an elevator down the side of the cañon—in short, to use this public pleasure ground as a means for private gain. There were half a dozen of us who, being very enthusiastic about the park, and, being in a position to watch legislation at Washington, and also to

NATIONAL PARK MOUNTAIN.

AT JUNCTION OF FIREHOLE AND GIBBON RIVERS.

know what was going on in the Interior Department, kept ourselves very much alive to the situation and succeeded in choking off half a dozen of these projects before they grew large enough to be made public.

One of these men was William Hallett Phillips, a dear friend of mine, a resident of Washington, a Supreme Court lawyer with a large acquaintance there, and a delightful fellow. He was the best co-worker that any one could have had who wanted to keep things straight and as they ought to be.

At rare intervals I get out old volumes of the *Forest and Stream* and look over the editorials written in those days with a mingling of amusement and sadness as I recall how excited we used to get, and think of the true fellows who used to help, but who have since crossed over to the other side.

Yours sincerely,

GEO. BIRD GRINNELL.

From *Forest and Stream,* August 20, 1904.

SENATOR VEST AND THE NATIONAL PARK.

In no one of all the editorials and obituaries written last week on the death of Senator Vest did we see mention made of one great service performed by him for the American people, and for which they and their descendants should always remember him. It is a bit of ancient history now, and largely forgotten by all except those who took an active part in the fight. More than twenty years ago strong efforts were made by a private corporation to secure a monopoly of the Yellowstone National Park by obtaining from the government, contracts giving them exclusive privileges within the Park. This corporation secured an agreement from the Interior Department by which six different plots in the Yellowstone Park, each one covering about one section of land— a square mile—were to be leased to it for a period of ten years. It was also to have a monopoly of hotel, stage and telegraph rights, and there was a privilege of renewal of the concession at the end of the ten years. The rate to be paid for the concession was $2 an acre.

When the question of this lease came before Congress, it was referred to a sub-committee of the Committee on Territories, of which Senator Vest was chairman. He investigated the question, and in the report made on it used these words: "Nothing but absolute necessity, however, should permit the Great National Park to be used for money-making by private persons, and, in our judgment, no such necessity exists. The purpose to which this region, matchless in wonders and grandeur, was dedicated—'a public park and a pleasure ground for the benefit and enjoyment of the people'—is worthy the highest patriotism and statesmanship."

The persons interested in this lease came from many sections of the country, and were ably represented by active agents in Washington. The pressure brought to bear on Congress was very great, and the more effectively applied, since few men knew much about conditions in the Yellowstone Park, or even where the Yellowstone Park was. But pressure and influence could not move Senator Vest when he knew he was right. He stood like a rock in Congress, resisting this pressure, making a noble fight in behalf of the interests of the people, and at last winning his battle. For years the issue seemed doubtful, and for years it was true that the sole hope of those who were devoted to the interests of the Park, and who were fighting the battle of the public, lay in Senator Vest. So after years of struggle the right triumphed, and the contract intended to be made between the Interior Department and the corporation was never consummated.

This long fight made evident the dangers to which the Park was exposed, and showed the necessity of additional legislation.

A bill to protect the Park was drawn by Senator Vest and passed by Congress, and from that time on, until the day of his retirement from public life, Senator Vest was ever a firm and watchful guardian of the Yellowstone National Park, showing in this matter, as in many others, "the highest patriotism and statesmanship." For many years, from 1882 to 1894, Senator Vest remained the chief defender of a National possession that self-seeking persons in many parts of the country were trying to use for their own profit.

W. Hallett Phillips

GEORGE GRAHAM VEST.

If we were asked to mention the two men who did more than any other two men to save the National Park for the American people, we should name George Graham Vest and William Hallett Phillips, co-workers in this good cause. There were other men who helped them, but these two easily stand foremost.   *   *   *   *   *   *

In the light of the present glorious development of the Park it can be said of each one who has taken part in the work of preserving for all time this great national pleasuring ground for the enjoyment of the American people, "He builded better than he knew."

An amusing feature of the identity of my name with the Park was that my friends, with a play upon my initials, frequently addressed letters to me in the following style:

The fame of the Yellowstone National Park, combining the most extensive aggregation of wonders in the world—wonders unexcelled because nowhere else existing—is now world-wide. The "Wonderland" publications issued by the Northern Pacific Railway, prepared under the careful supervision of their author, Olin D. Wheeler, with their superb illustrations of the natural scenery of the park, and the illustrated volume, "The Yellowstone," by Major Hiram M. Chittenden, U. S. Engineers, under whose direction the roads and bridges throughout the Park are being construct-

ed, have so confirmed the first accounts of these wonders
that there remains now little of the incredulity with which
the narrations of the members of our company were first
received. The articles written by me on my return from
the trip described in this diary, and published in Scribner's
(now Century) Magazine for May and June, 1871, were regarded more as the amiable exaggerations of an enthusiastic Munchausen, who is disposed to tell the whole truth,
and as much more as is necessary to make an undoubted
sensation, than as the story of a sober, matter-of-fact observer who tells what he has seen with his own eyes, and
exaggerates nothing. Dr. Holland, one of the editors of
that magazine, sent to me a number of uncomplimentary
criticisms of my article. One reviewer said: "This Langford must be the champion liar of the Northwest." Resting for a time under this imputation, I confess to a feeling
of satisfaction in reading from a published letter, written
later in the summer of 1871 from the Upper Geyser basin
by a member of the U. S. Geological Survey, the words:
"Langford did not dare tell one-half of what he saw."

Mr. Charles T. Whitmell, of Cardiff, Wales, a distinguished scholar and astronomer, who has done much to
bring to the notice of our English brothers the wonders of
the Park—which he visited in 1883—in a lecture delivered
before the Cardiff Naturalists' Society on Nov. 12, 1885,
sought to impress upon the minds of his audience the full
significance of the above characterization. He said: "This
quite unique description means a great deal, I can assure
you; for Western American lying is not to be measured by
any of our puny European standards of untruthfulness."

But the writings of Wheeler and others, running through
a long series of years and covering an extended range of new
discoveries, have vindicated the truthfulness of the early
explorers, and even the stories of Bridger are not now re-

garded as exaggerations, and we no longer write for his epitaph,

Here LIES Bridger.

As I recall the events of this exploration, made thirty-five years ago, it is a pleasure to bear testimony that there was never a more unselfish or generous company of men associated for such an expedition; and, notwithstanding the importance of our discoveries, in the honor of which each desired to have his just share, there was absolutely neither jealousy nor ungenerous rivalry, and the various magazine and newspaper articles first published clearly show how the members of our party were "In honor preferring one another."

In reviewing my diary, preparatory to its publication, I have occasionally eliminated an expression that seemed to be too personal,—a sprinkling of pepper from the caster of my impatience,—and I have also here and there added an explanatory annotation or illustration. With this exception I here present the original notes just as they were penned under the inspiration of the overwhelming wonders which everywhere revealed themselves to our astonished vision; and as I again review and read the entries made in the field and around the campfire, in the journal that for nearly thirty years has been lost to my sight, I feel all the thrilling sensations of my first impressions, and with them is mingled the deep regret that our beloved Washburn did not live to see the triumphant accomplishment of what was dear to his heart, the setting apart at the headwaters of the Yellowstone, of a National "public park or pleasuring ground for the benefit and enjoyment of the people."

NATHANIEL PITT LANGFORD.

St. Paul, Minn., August 9, 1905.

The Author

JOURNAL

Wednesday, August 17, 1870.—In accordance with the arrangements made last night, the different members of our party met at the agreed rendezvous—the office of General Washburn—at 9 o'clock a. m., to complete our arrangements for the journey and get under way. Our party consisted of Gen. Henry D. Washburn, Cornelius Hedges, Samuel T. Hauser, Warren C. Gillette, Benjamin Stickney, Truman C. Everts, Walter Trumbull, Jacob Smith and Nathaniel P. Langford. General Washburn has been chosen the leader of our party. For assistants we have Mr. —————— Reynolds and Elwyn Bean, western slope packers, and two African boys as cooks. Each man has a saddle horse fully rigged with California saddle, cantinas, holsters, etc., and has furnished a pack horse for transportation of provisions, ammunition and blankets. There are but few of our party who are adepts in the art of packing, for verily it is an art acquired by long practice, and we look with admiration upon our packers as they "throw the rope" with such precision, and with great skill and rapidity tighten the cinch and gird the load securely upon the back of the broncho. Our ponies have not all been tried of late with the pack saddle, but most of them quietly submit to the loading.   But now comes one that does not yield itself to the manipulations of the packer. He stands quiet till the pack saddle is adjusted, but the moment he feels the tightening of the cinch he asserts his independence of all restraint and commences bucking.   This ani-

PACKING A RECALCITRANT MULE.

mal in question belongs to Gillette, who says that if he does not stand the pack he will use him for a saddle horse.   If so, God save Gillette!

Thursday, August 18.—I rode on ahead of the party from Mr. Hartzell's ranch, stopping at Radersburg for dinner and riding through a snow storm to Gallatin City, where I remained over night with Major Campbell.   General Washburn thought that it would be well for some members of the company to have a conference, as early as possible, with the commanding officer at Fort Ellis, concerning an escort of soldiers. I also desired to confer with some of the members of the Bozeman Masonic Lodge concerning the lodge troubles; and it was for these reasons that I rode on to Bozeman in advance of the party.

THE START.

PRICKLY PEAR VALLEY.

Friday, August 19.—Rode over to the East Gallatin river with Lieutenants Batchelor and Wright, crossing at Blakeley's bridge and reaching Bozeman at 7 o'clock p. m.

Saturday, August 20.—Spent the day at Bozeman and at Fort Ellis. I met the commanding officer, Major Baker, of the Second U. S. Cavalry, who informs me that nearly all the men of his command are in the field fighting the Indians.

I informed him that we had an order for an escort of soldiers, and he said that the garrison was so weakened that he could not spare more than half a dozen men. I told him that six men added to our own roster would enable us to do good guard duty. The rest of the party and the pack train came into Bozeman at night.

This evening I visited Gallatin Lodge No. 6, and after a full consultation with its principal officers and members, I reluctantly decided to exercise my prerogative as Grand Master and arrest the charter of the lodge as the only means of bringing to a close a grievous state of dissension. In justice to my own convictions of duty, I could not have adopted any milder remedy than the one I applied.

Sunday, August 21.—We moved into camp about one-half mile from Fort Ellis on the East Gallatin. General Washburn presented the order of Major General Hancock (recommended by General Baird, Inspector General, as an important military necessity) for an escort. Major Baker repeated what he said to me yesterday, and he will detail for our service five soldiers under the command of a lieutenant, and we are satisfied. General Lester Willson entertained us at a bounteous supper last night. His wife is a charming musician.

Monday, August 22.—We left Fort Ellis at 11 o'clock this forenoon with an escort consisting of five men under command of Lieut. Gustavus C. Doane of the Second U. S. Cavalry. Lieutenant Doane has kindly allowed me to copy the special order detailing him for this service. It is as follows:

Headquarters Fort Ellis, Montana Territory,
August 21, 1870.

In accordance with instructions from Headquarters District of Montana, Lieutenant G. C. Doane, Second Cavalry, will proceed with one sergeant and four privates of Company F. Second Cavalry, to escort the Surveyor General of

Olin D Wheeler

Montana to the falls and lakes of the Yellowstone, and return. They will be supplied with thirty days' rations, and one hundred rounds of ammunition per man. The acting assistant quarter-master will furnish them with the necessary transportation.

By order of Major Baker.

J. G. MacADAMS,
First Lieutenant Second Cavalry.
Acting Post Adjutant.

The names of the soldiers are Sergeant William Baker and Privates John Williamson, George W. McConnell, William Leipler and Charles Moore. This number, added to our own company of nine, will give us fourteen men for guard duty, a sufficient number to maintain a guard of two at all times, with two reliefs each night, each man serving half of a night twice each week. Our entire number, including the packers and cooks, is nineteen (19).

Along the trail, after leaving Fort Ellis, we found large quantities of the "service" berry, called by the Snake Indians "Tee-amp." Our ascent of the Belt range was somewhat irregular, leading us up several sharp acclivities, until we attained at the summit an elevation of nearly two thousand feet above the valley we had left. The scene from this point is excelled in grandeur only by extent and variety. An amphitheatre of mountains 200 miles in circumference, enclosing a valley nearly as large as the State of Rhode Island, with all its details of pinnacle, peak, dome, rock and river, is comprehended at a glance. In front of us at a distance of twenty miles, in sullen magnificence, rose the picturesque range of the Madison, with the insulated rock, Mount Washington, and the sharp pinnacle of Ward's Peak prominently in the foreground. Following the range to the right for the distance of twenty-five miles, the eye rests upon that singular depression where, formed by the confluent streams of the Madison, Jefferson and Gallatin, the mighty Missouri commences its meanderings to the Gulf. Far beyond these, in full blue outline, are defined the round knobs of the Boulder mountains, stretching away and imperceptibly commingling with the distant horizon. At the left, towering a thousand feet above the circumjacent ranges, are the glowering peaks of the Yellowstone, their summits half enveloped in clouds, or glittering with perpetual snow. At our feet, apparently within jumping distance, cleft centrally by its arrowy river, carpeted with verdure, is the magnificent valley of the Gallatin, like a rich emerald in its gorgeous mountain setting. Fascinating as was this scene we gave it but a glance, and turned our horses' heads towards the vast unknown. Descending the range to the east, we reached Trail creek, a tributary of the Yellowstone, about 3 o'clock in the afternoon, where we are now camped for the night. We are now fairly launched upon our expedition without the possibility of obtaining outside assistance in case we need it, and means for our protection have been fully considered since we camped, and our plans for guard duty throughout the trip have been arranged. Hedges is to be my comrade-in-arms in this service. He has expressed to me his great satisfaction that he is to be associated with me throughout the trip in this night guard duty, and I am especially pleased at being assigned to duty with so reliable a coadjutor as Hedges, a man who can be depended upon to neglect no duty. We two are to stand guard the first half of this first night—that is, until 1 o'clock to-morrow morning; then Washburn and Hauser take our places. Fresh Indian signs indicate that the red-skins are lurking near us, and justify the apprehensions expressed in the letter which Hauser and I received from James Stuart, that we will be attacked by the Crow Indians.* I am not entirely free from anxiety. Our safety

---

*In his diary under date of August 22d General Washburn wrote: "Stood guard. Quite cold. Crows (Indians) near."

will depend upon our vigilance. We are all well armed with long range repeating rifles and needle guns, though there are but few of our party who are experts at off-hand shooting with a revolver.

In the course of our discussion Jake Smith expressed his doubt whether any member of our party except Hauser (who

TAKING A SHOT AT JAKE SMITH'S HAT.

is an expert pistol shot) is sufficiently skilled in the use of the revolver to hit an Indian at even a close range, and he offered to put the matter to a test by setting up his hat at a distance of twenty yards for the boys to shoot at with their revolvers, without a rest, at twenty-five cents a shot. While

several members of our party were blazing away with indifferent success, with the result that Jake was adding to his
exchequer without damage to his hat, I could not resist the
inclination to quietly drop out of sight behind a clump of
bushes, where from my place of concealment I sent from
my breech-loading Ballard repeating rifle four bullets in
rapid succession, through the hat, badly riddling it.   Jake
inquired, "Whose revolver is it that makes that loud report?" He did not discover the true state of the case, but
removed the target with the ready acknowledgment that
there were members of our party whose aim with a revolver
was more accurate than he had thought.   I think that I will
make confession to him in a few days.   I now wish that I
had brought with me an extra hat.   My own is not large
enough for Jake's head.   Notwithstanding the serious problems which we must deal with in making this journey, it is
well to have a little amusement while we may.

Tuesday, August 23.—Last night was the first that we
were on guard.   The first relief was Hedges and Langford,
the second Washburn and Hauser.   Everything went well.
At 8 a. m. to-day we broke camp.   Some delay occurring in
packing our horses, Lieutenant Doane and the escort went
ahead, and we did not again see them until we reached our
night camp.

We traveled down Trail creek and over a spur of the mountain to the valley of the Yellowstone, which we followed up
eight miles to our present camp.   Along on our right in passing up the valley was a vast natural pile of basaltic rock,
perpendicular, a part of which had been overthrown, showing transverse seams in the rock.   Away at the right in the
highest range bordering the valley was Pyramid mountain,
itself a snow-capped peak; and further up the range was
a long ridge covered with deep snow.   As we passed Pyramid mountain a cloud descended upon it, casting its gloomy

shadow over the adjacent peaks and bursting in a grand storm. These magnificent changes in mountain scenery occasioned by light and shade during one of these terrific tempests, with all the incidental accompaniments of thunder, lightning, rain, snow and hail, afford the most awe-inspiring exhibition in nature. As I write, another grand storm, which does not extend to our camp, has broken out on Emigrant peak, which at one moment is completely obscured in darkness; at the next, perhaps, brilliant with light; all its gorges, recesses, seams and cañons illuminated; these fade away into dim twilight, broken by a terrific flash, and, echoing to successive peals,

"*   *   * the rattling crags among

Leaps the live thunder" in innumerable reverberations.

On the left of the valley the foot hills were mottled with a carpet of beautiful, maroon-colored, delicately-tinted verdure, and towering above all rose peak on peak of the snow-capped mountains.

To-day we saw our first Indians as we descended into the valley of the Yellowstone. They came down from the east side of the valley, over the foot hills, to the edge of the plateau overlooking the bottom lands of the river, and there conspicuously displayed themselves for a time to engage our attention. As we passed by them up the valley they moved down to where their ponies were hobbled. Two of our party, Hauser and Stickney, had dropped behind and passed towards the north to get a shot at an antelope; and when they came up they reported that, while we were observing the Indians on the plateau across the river, there were one hundred or more of them watching us from behind a high butte as our pack-train passed up the valley. As soon as they observed Hauser and Stickney coming up nearly behind them, they wheeled their horses and disappeared down the other side of the butte.*   This early admonition of our exposure to hostile attack, and liability to be robbed of everything, and compelled on foot and without provisions to retrace our steps, has been the subject of discussion in our camp to-night. and has renewed in our party the deter-

ON GUARD.

VALLEY OF THE YELLOWSTONE.

mination to abate nothing of our vigilance, and keep in a condition of constant preparation.

With our long-range rifles and plenty of ammunition, we can stand off 200 or 300 of them, with their less efficient weapons, if we don't let them sneak up upon us in the night. If we encounter more than that number, then what? The odds will be against us that they will "rub us out," as Jim Stuart says.

---

*On August 23d General Washburn wrote: "Indians of the Crow tribe."

Jake Smith has sent the first demoralizing shot into the camp by announcing that he doesn't think there is any necessity for standing guard.   Jake is the only one of our party who shows some sign of baldness, and he probably thinks that his own scalp is not worth the taking by the Indians.

Did we act wisely in permitting him to join our party at the last moment before leaving Helena?   One careless man, no less than one who is easily discouraged by difficulties, will frequently demoralize an entire company.   I think we have now taken all possible precautions for our safety, but our numbers are few; and for me to say that I am not in hourly dread of the Indians when they appear in large force, would be a braggart boast.

Mr. Everts was taken sick this afternoon.   All day we have had a cool breeze and a few light showers, clearing off from time to time, revealing the mountains opposite us covered from their summits half way down with the newly fallen snow, and light clouds floating just below over the foot hills.   Until we reached the open valley of the Yellowstone our route was over a narrow trail, from which the stream, Trail creek, takes its name.   The mountains opposite the point where we entered the valley are rugged, grand, picturesque and immense by turns, and colored by nature with a thousand gorgeous hues.   We have traveled all this day amid this stupendous variety of landscape until we have at length reached the western shore of that vast and solitary river which is to guide us to the theatre of our explorations.   From the "lay of the land" I should judge that our camp to-night is thirty-five to forty miles above the point where Captain William Clark, of the famous Lewis and Clark expedition, embarked with his party in July, 1806, in two cottonwood canoes bound together with buffalo thongs, on his return to the states.   It was from that point also that some six hundred residents of Montana embarked for a trip to the states, in forty-two flat boats, in the autumn of 1865.*   We learn from Mr. Boteler that there are some twenty-five lodges of Crow Indians up the valley.*

Wednesday, August 24.—It rained nearly all of last night, but Lieutenant Doane pitched his large tent, which was sufficiently capacious to accommodate us all by lying "heads and tails," and we were very comfortable.   Throughout the forenoon we had occasional showers, but about noon it cleared away, and, after getting a lunch, we got under way. During the forenoon some of the escort were very success-ful in fishing for trout.   Mr. Everts was not well enough to accompany us, and it was arranged that he should remain at Boteler's ranch, and that we would move about twelve miles up the river, and there await his arrival.   Our prepa-rations for departure being completed, General Washburn detailed a guard of four men to accompany the pack train, while the rest of the party rode on ahead.   We broke camp at 2:30 p. m. with the pack train and moved up the valley. At about six miles from our camp we crossed a spur of the mountain which came down boldly to the river, and from the top we had a beautiful view of the valley stretched out below us, the stream fringed with a thin bordering of trees, the foot hills rising into a level plateau covered with rich bunch grass, and towering above all, the snow-covered sum-mits of the distant mountains rising majestically, seem-ingly just out of the plateau, though they were many miles

---

*Near where Livingston is now located.

---

*Lieutenant Doane in his report to the War Department under date of August 24th writes: "Guards were established here during the night, as there were signs of a party of Indians on the trail ahead of us, all the members of the party taking their tours of this duty, and using in addition the various precautions of lariats, hob-bles, etc., not to be neglected while traveling through this country."

away. Above us the valley opened out wide, and from the overlooking rock on which we stood we could see the long train of pack horses winding their way along the narrow trail, the whole presenting a picturesque scene. The rock on which we stood was a coarse conglomerate, or pudding stone.

Five miles farther on we crossed a small stream bordered with black cherry trees, many of the smaller ones broken down by bears, of which animal we found many signs. One mile farther on we made our camp about a mile below the middle cañon. To-night we have antelope, rabbit, duck, grouse and the finest of large trout for supper. As I write, General Washburn, Hedges and Hauser are engaged in an animated discussion of the differences between France and Germany, and the probabilities of the outcome of the war. The three gentlemen are not agreed in determining where the responsibility for the trouble lies, and I fear that I will have to check their profanity. However, neither Washburn nor Hedges swears.

Thursday, August 25.—Last night was very cold, the thermometer marking 40 degrees at 8 o'clock a. m. At one mile of travel we came to the middle cañon, which we passed on a very narrow trail running over a high spur of the mountain overlooking the river, which at this point is forced through a narrow gorge, surging and boiling and tumbling over the rocks, the water having a dark green color. After passing the cañon we again left the valley, passing over the mountain, on the top of which at an elevation of several hundred feet above the river is a beautiful lake. Descending the mountain again, we entered the valley, which here is about one and a half to two miles wide. At nineteen miles from our morning camp we came to Gardiner's river, at the mouth of which we camped. We are near the southern boundary of Montana, and still in the limestone and

granite formations. Mr. Everts came into camp just at night, nearly recovered, but very tired from his long and tedious ride over a rugged road, making our two days' travel in one. We passed to-day a singular formation which we named "The Devil's Slide." From the top of the mountain to the valley, a distance of about 800 feet, the trap rock projected from 75 to 125 feet, the intermediate layers of friable rock having been washed out. The trap formation is about twenty-five feet wide, and covered with stunted pine trees. Opposite our camp is a high drift formation of granite boulders, gravel and clay. The boulders are the regular gray Quincy granite, and those in the middle of the river are hollowed out by the action of the water into many curious shapes. We have here found our first specimens of petrifactions and obsidian, or volcanic glass. From the top of the mountain back of our camp we can see to-night a smoke rising from another peak, which some of our party think is a signal from one band of the Indians to another, conveying intelligence of our progress. Along our trail of to-day are plenty of Indian "signs," and marks of the lodge poles dragging in the sand on either side of the trail.*

Jake Smith stood guard last night, or ought to have done so, and but for the fact that Gillette was also on guard, I should not have had an undisturbed sleep. We know that the Indians are near us, and sleep is more refreshing to me when I feel assured that I will not be joined in my slumbers by those who are assigned for watchful guard duty.

---

*Under date of August 25th Lieutenant Doane writes: "From this camp was seen the smoke of fires on the mountains in front, while Indian signs became more numerous and distinct." Under date of August 25th General Washburn wrote in his diary: "Have been following Indian trails, fresh ones, all the way. They are about two days ahead of us."

Friday, August 26.—For some reason we did not leave camp till 11 o'clock a. m. We forded Gardiner's river with some difficulty, several of our pack animals being nearly carried off their feet by the torrent. We passed over several rocky ridges or points coming down from the mountain, and at one and a half miles came down again into the valley, which one of our party called the "Valley of desolation." Taking the trail upon the left, we followed it until it led us to the mouth of a cañon, through which ran an old Indian or game trail, which was hardly discernible, and had evidently been long abandoned. Retracing our steps for a quarter of a mile, and taking a cut-off through the sage brush, we followed another trail upon our right up through a steep, dry coulee. From the head of the coulee we went through fallen timber over a burnt and rocky road, our progress being very slow. A great many of the packs came off our horses or became loosened, necessitating frequent haltings for their readjustment. Upon the summit we found a great many shells. Descending the divide we found upon the trail the carcass of an antelope which the advance party had killed, and which we packed on our horses and carried to our night camp. In the morning Lieutenant Doane and one of his men, together with Mr. Everts, had started out ahead of the party to search out the best trail. At 3 o'clock p. m. we arrived at Antelope creek, only six miles from our morning camp, where we concluded to halt. On the trail which we were following there were no tracks except those of unshod ponies; and, as our horses were all shod, it was evident that Lieutenant Doane and the advance party had descended the mountain by some other trail than that which we were following. Neither were there any marks of dragging lodge poles. There are seemingly two trails across the mountain,—a circuitous one by as easy a grade as can be found, over which the Indians send their families with their heavily laden pack horses; and a more direct, though more difficult, route which the war parties use in making their rapid rides. This last is the one we have taken, and the advance party has doubtless taken the other.

Our camp to-night is on Antelope creek, about five miles from the Yellowstone river. After our arrival in camp, in company with Stickney and Gillette, I made a scout of eight or ten miles through the country east of our trail, and between it and the river, in search of some sign of Lieutenant Doane, but we found no trace of him. Parting from Stickney and Gillette, I followed down the stream through a narrow gorge by a game trail, hoping if I could reach the Yellowstone, to find a good trail along its banks up to the foot of the Grand cañon; but I found the route impracticable for the passage of our pack train. After supper Mr. Hauser and I went out in search of our other party, and found the tracks of their horses, which we followed about four miles to the brow of a mountain overlooking the country for miles in advance of us. Here we remained an hour, firing our guns as a signal, and carefully scanning the whole country with our field glasses. We could discern the trail for many miles on its tortuous course, but could see no sign of a camp, or of horses feeding, and we returned to our camp.

Saturday, August 27.—Lieutenant Doane and those who were with him did not return to camp last night. At change of guard Gillette's pack horse became alarmed at something in the bushes bordering upon the creek on the bank of which he was tied, and, breaking loose, dashed through the camp, rousing all of us. Some wild animal—snake, fox or something of the kind—was probably the cause of the alarm. In its flight I became entangled in the lariat and was dragged head first for three or four rods, my head striking a log, which proved to be very rotten, and offered little resistance to a hard head, and did me very little damage.   Towards morning a slight shower of rain fell, continuing at intervals till 8 o'clock.   We left camp about 9 o'clock, the pack train following about 11 o'clock, and soon struck the trail of Lieutenant Doane, which proved to be the route traveled by the Indians.   The marks of their lodge poles were plainly visible.   At about four miles from our morning camp we discovered at some distance ahead of us what first appeared to be a young elk, but which proved to be a colt that had become separated from the camp of Indians to which it belonged.   We think the Indians cannot be far from us at this time.   Following the trail up the ascent leading from Antelope creek, we entered a deep cut, the sides of which rise at an angle of 45 degrees, and are covered with a luxuriant growth of grass.   Through this cut we ascended by a grade entirely practicable for a wagon road to the summit of the divide separating the waters of Antelope creek from those of *—— creek, and from the summit descended through a beautiful gorge to a small tributary of the Yellowstone, a distance of two miles, dismounting and leading our horses almost the entire distance, the descent being too precipitous for the rider's comfort or for ease to the horse.   We were now within four miles of *—— creek, and within two miles of the Yellowstone.   On the right of the trail, two miles farther on, we found a small hot sulphur spring, the water of which was at a temperature a little below the boiling point, which at this elevation is about 195 degrees.   Ascending a high ridge we had a commanding view of a basaltic formation of palisades, about

---

*These blanks were left in my diary with the intention of filling them, upon the selection by our party of a name for the creek; but after going into camp at Tower fall, the matter of selecting a name was forgotten. A few years later the stream was named Lost creek.

thirty feet in height, on the opposite bank of the Yellowstone, overlooking a stratum of cement and gravel nearly two hundred feet thick, beneath which is another formation of the basaltic rock, and beneath this another body of cement and gravel. We named this formation "Column Rock." The upper formation, from which the rock takes its name, consists of basaltic columns about thirty feet high, closely touching each other, the columns being from three to five feet in diameter. A little farther on we descended the sides of the cañon, through which runs a large creek. We crossed this creek and camped on the south side. Our camp is about four hundred feet in elevation above the Yellowstone, which is not more than two miles distant. The creek is full of granite boulders, varying in size from six inches to ten feet in diameter.

General Washburn was on guard last night, and to-night he seems somewhat fatigued. Mr. Hedges has improvised a writing stool from a sack of flour, and I have appropriated a sack of beans for a like use; and, as we have been writing, there has been a lively game of cards played near my left side, which Hedges, who has just closed his diary, says is a game of poker. I doubt if Deacon Hedges is sufficiently posted in the game to know to a certainty that poker is the game which is being played; but, putting what Hedges tells me with what I see and hear, I find that these infatuated players have put a valuation of five (5) cents per bean, on beans that did not cost more than $1 a quart in Helena, and Jake Smith exhibits a marvelous lack of veneration for his kinswoman, by referring to each bean, as he places it before him upon the table, as his "aunt," or, more flippantly, his "auntie." Walter Trumbull has been styled the "Banker," and he says that at the commencement of the game he sold forty of these beans to each of the players, himself included (200 in all), at five (5) cents each, and that he has already redeemed the entire 200 at that rate; and now Jake Smith has a half-pint cup nearly full of beans, and is demanding of Trumbull that he redeem them also; that is, pay five (5) cents per bean for the contents of the cup. Trumbull objects. Jake persists. Reflecting upon their disagreement I recall that about an hour ago Jake, with an apologetic "Excuse me!" disturbed me while I was writing and untied the bean sack on which I am now sitting, and took from it a double handful of beans.

It seems to me that a game of cards which admits of such latitude as this, with a practically unlimited draft upon outside resources, is hardly fair to all parties, and especially to "The Banker."

Sunday, August 28.—To-day being Sunday, we remained all day in our camp, which Washburn and Everts have named "Camp Comfort," as we have an abundance of venison and trout.

We visited the falls of the creek, the waters of which tumble over the rocks and boulders for the distance of 200 yards from our camp, and then fall a distance of 110 feet, as triangulated by Mr. Hauser. Stickney ventured to the verge of the fall, and, with a stone attached to a strong cord, measured its height, which he gives as 105 feet.

The stream, in its descent to the brink of the fall, is separated into half a dozen distorted channels which have zigzagged their passage through the cement formation, working it into spires, pinnacles, towers and many other capricious objects. Many of these are of faultless symmetry, resembling the minaret of a mosque; others are so grotesque as to provoke merriment as well as wonder. One of this latter character we named "The Devil's Hoof," from its supposed similarity to the proverbial foot of his Satanic majesty. The height of this rock from its base is about fifty feet.

The friable rock forming the spires and towers and pinnacles crumbles away under a slight pressure. I climbed
one of these tall spires on the brink of the chasm overlooking the fall, and from the top had a beautiful view, though
it was one not unmixed with terror. Directly beneath my
feet, but probably about one hundred feet below me, was

DEVIL'S HOOF.

the verge of the fall, and still below that the deep gorge
through which the creek went bounding and roaring over
the boulders to its union with the Yellowstone. The scenery
here cannot be called grand or magnificent, but it is most
beautiful and picturesque. The spires are from 75 to 100
feet in height. The volume of water is about six or eight

times that of Minnehaha fall, and I think that a month ago, while the snows were still melting, the creek could not easily have been forded. The route to the foot of the fall is by a well worn Indian trail running to the mouth of the creek over boulders and fallen pines, and through thickets of raspberry bushes.

At the mouth of the creek on the Yellowstone is a hot sulphur spring, the odor from which is perceptible in our camp to-day. At the base of the fall we found a large petrifaction of wood imbedded in the debris of the falling cement and slate rock. There are several sulphur springs at the mouth of the creek, three of them boiling, others nearly as hot as boiling water. There is also a milky white sulphur spring. Within one yard of a spring, the temperature of which is little below the boiling point, is a sulphur spring with water nearly as cold as ice water, or not more than ten degrees removed from it.

I went around and almost under the fall, or as far as the rocks gave a foot-hold, the rising spray thoroughly wetting and nearly blinding me. Some two hundred yards below the fall is a huge granite boulder about thirty feet in diameter. Where did it come from?

In camp to-day several names were proposed for the creek and fall, and after much discussion the name "Minaret" was selected. Later, this evening, this decision has been reconsidered, and we have decided to substitute the name "Tower" for "Minaret," and call it "Tower Fall."*

---

*In making a copy of my original diary, it is proper at this point to interpolate an account of the circumstances under which the name "Tower" was bestowed upon the creek and fall.

At the outset of our journey we had agreed that we would not give to any object of interest which we might discover the name of any of our party nor of our friends. This rule was to be religiously observed. While in camp on Sunday, August 28th, on the bank of this creek, it was suggested that we select a name for the creek and fall. Walter Trumbull suggested "Minaret Creek" and

General Washburn rode out to make a *reconnaissance* for a route to the river, and returned about 3 o'clock in the afternoon with the intelligence that from the summit of a high mountain he had seen Yellowstone lake, the proposed object of our visit; and with his compass he had noted its direction from our camp. This intelligence has greatly relieved our anxiety concerning the course we are to pursue, and has quieted the dread apprehensions of some of our number, lest we become inextricably involved in the wooded labyrinth by which we are surrounded; and in violation of our agreement that we would not give the name of any member of our party to any object of interest, we have spontaneously and by unanimous vote given the mountain the name by which it will hereafter and forever be known, "Mount Washburn."

In addition to our saddle horses and pack horses, we have another four-footed animal in our outfit—a large black dog of seeming little intelligence, to which we have given the

---

"Minaret Fall." Mr. Hauser suggested "Tower Creek" and "Tower Fall." After some discussion a vote was taken, and by a small majority the name "Minaret" was decided upon. During the following evening Mr. Hauser stated with great seriousness that he had violated the agreement made relative to naming objects for our friends. He said that the well known Southern family—the Rhetts—lived in St. Louis, and that they had a most charming and accomplished daughter named "Minnie." He said that this daughter was a sweetheart of Trumbull, who had proposed the name— her name—"Minnie Rhett"—and that we had unwittingly given to the fall and creek the name of this sweetheart of Mr. Trumbull. Mr. Trumbull indignantly denied the truth of Hauser's statement, and Hauser as determinedly insisted that it was the truth, and the vote was therefore reconsidered, and by a substantial majority it was decided to substitute the name "Tower" for "Minaret." Later, and when it was too late to recall or reverse the action of our party, it was surmised that Hauser himself had a sweetheart in St. Louis, a Miss Tower. Some of our party, Walter Trumbull especially, always insisted that such was the case. The weight of testimony was so evenly balanced that I shall hesitate long before I believe either side of this part of the story.

N. P. LANGFORD.

name of "Booby." He is owned by "Nute," one of our colored boys, who avers that he is a very knowing dog, and
will prove himself so before our journey is ended. The
poor beast is becoming sore-footed, and his sufferings excite
our sympathy, and we are trying to devise some kind of
shoe or moccasin for him. The rest to-day in camp will
benefit him. Lieutenant Doane is suffering greatly with a
felon on his thumb. It ought to be opened, but he is unwilling to submit to a thorough operation. His sufferings
kept him awake nearly all of last night.

Monday, August 29.—We broke camp about 8 o'clock,
leaving the trail, which runs down to the mouth of the
creek, and passed over a succession of high ridges, and part
of the time through fallen timber. The trail of the Indians
leads off to the left, to the brink of the Yellowstone, which
it follows up about three-fourths of a mile, and then crosses
to the east side. Hauser, Gillette, Stickney, Trumbull and
myself rode out to the summit of Mount Washburn, which
is probably the highest peak on the west side of the river.
Having an aneroid barometer with us, we ascertained the
elevation of the mountain to be about 9,800 feet. The summit is about 500 feet above the snow line.

Descending the mountain on the southwest side, we came
upon the trail of the pack train, which we followed to our
camp at the head of a small stream running into the Yellowstone, which is about five miles distant. As we came
into camp a black bear kindly vacated the premises. After
supper some of our party followed down the creek to its
mouth. At about one mile below our camp the creek runs
through a bed of volcanic ashes, which extends for a hundred yards on either side. Toiling on our course down this
creek to the river we came suddenly upon a basin of boiling
sulphur springs, exhibiting signs of activity and points of
difference so wonderful as to fully absorb our curiosity.

The largest of these, about twenty feet in diameter, is boiling like a cauldron, throwing water and fearful volumes of sulphurous vapor higher than our heads. Its color is a disagreeable greenish yellow. The central spring of the group, of dark leaden hue, is in the most violent agitation, its convulsive spasms frequently projecting large masses of water to the height of seven or eight feet. The spring lying to the east of this, more diabolical in appearance, filled with a hot brownish substance of the consistency of mucilage, is in constant noisy ebullition, emitting fumes of villainous odor. Its surface is covered with bubbles, which are constantly rising and bursting, and emitting sulphurous gases from various parts of its surface. Its appearance has suggested the name, which Hedges has given, of "Hell-Broth springs;" for, as we gazed upon the infernal mixture and inhaled the pungent sickening vapors, we were impressed with the idea that this was a most perfect realization of Shakespeare's image in Macbeth. It needed but the presence of Hecate and her weird band to realize that horrible creation of poetic fancy, and I fancied the "black and midnight hags" concocting a charm around this horrible cauldron. We ventured near enough to this spring to dip the end of a pine pole into it, which, upon removal, was covered an eighth of an inch thick with lead-colored sulphury slime.

There are five large springs and half a dozen smaller ones in this basin, all of them strongly impregnated with sulphur, alum and arsenic. The water from all the larger springs is dark brown or nearly black. The largest spring is fifteen to eighteen feet in diameter, and the water boils up like a cauldron from 18 to 30 inches, and one instinctively draws back from the edge as the hot sulphur steam rises around him. Another of the larger springs is intermittent. The smaller springs are farther up on the bank than the larger ones. The deposit of sinter bordering one of them, with the emission of steam and smoke combined, gives it a resemblance to a chimney of a miner's cabin. Around them all is an incrustation formed from the bases of the spring deposits, arsenic, alum, sulphur, etc. This incrustation is sufficiently strong in many places to bear the weight of a man, but more frequently it gave way, and from

SECURING A SPECIMEN
AT HELL-BROTH SPRINGS.

the apertures thus created hot steam issued, showing it to be dangerous to approach the edge of the springs; and it was with the greatest difficulty that I obtained specimens of the incrustation. This I finally accomplished by lying at full length upon that portion of the incrustation which yielded the least, but which was not sufficiently strong to bear my weight while I stood upright, and at imminent risk of sinking in the infernal mixture, I rolled over and over to the edge of the opening; and, with the crust slowly bending and sinking beneath me, hurriedly secured the coveted prize of black sulphur, and rolled back to a place of safety.

From the springs to the mouth of the creek we followed along the bank, the bed or bottom being too rough and precipitous for us to travel in it, the total fall in the creek for the three miles being about fifteen hundred feet. Standing upon the high point at the junction of the creek with the Yellowstone, one first gets some idea of the depth of the cañon through which the river runs. From this height the sound of the waters of the Yellowstone, tumbling over tremendous rocks and boulders, could not be heard. Everything around us—mountains, valleys, cañon and trees, heights and depths—all are in such keeping and proportion that all our estimates of distances are far below the real truth. To-day we passed the mouth of Hell-Roaring river on the opposite side of the Yellowstone.

It was again Jake Smith's turn for guard duty last night, but this morning Jake's countenance wore a peculiar expression, which indicated that he possessed some knowledge not shared by the rest of the party. He spoke never a word, and was as serene as a Methodist minister behind four aces. My interpretation of this self-satisfied serenity is that his guard duty did not deprive him of much sleep. When it comes to considering the question of danger in this Indian country, Jake thinks that he knows more than the veteran Jim Stuart, whom we expected to join us on this trip, and who has given us some salutary words of caution. In a matter in which the safety of our whole party is involved, it is unfortunate that there are no "articles of war" to aid in the enforcement of discipline, in faithful guard duty.

Tuesday, August 30.—We broke camp about 9 o'clock a. m., traveling in a southerly direction over the hills adjoining our camp, and then descended the ridge in a southwesterly direction, heading off several ravines, till we came into a small valley; thence we crossed over a succession of ridges of fallen timber to a creek, where we halted about ten miles from our morning camp and about a mile from the upper fall of the Yellowstone. Mr. Hedges gave the name "Cascade creek" to this stream.

When we left our camp this morning at Hell-Broth springs, I remarked to Mr. Hedges and General Washburn that the wonders of which we were in pursuit had not disappointed us in their first exhibitions, and that I was encouraged in the faith that greater curiosities lay before us. We believed that the great cataracts of the Yellowstone were within two days', or at most three days', travel. So when we reached Cascade creek, on which we are now encamped, after a short day of journeying, it was with much astonishment as well as delight that we found ourselves in the immediate presence of the falls. Their roar, smothered by the vast depth of the cañon into which they plunge, was not heard until they were before us. With remarkable deliberation we unsaddled and lariated our horses, and even refreshed ourselves with such creature comforts as our larder readily afforded, before we deigned a survey of these great wonders of nature. On our walk down the creek to the river, struck with the beauty of its cascades, we even neglected the greater, to admire the lesser wonders. Rushing with great celerity through a deep defile of lava and obsidian, worn into caverns and fissures, the stream, one-fourth of a mile from its debouchure, breaks into a continuous cascade of remarkable beauty, consisting of a fall of five feet, succeeded by another of fifteen into a grotto formed by proximate rocks imperfectly arching it, whence from a crystal pool of unfathomable depth at their base, it lingers as if half reluctant to continue its course, or as if to renew its power, and then glides gracefully over a descending, almost perpendicular, ledge, veiling the rocks for the distance of eighty feet. Mr. Hedges gave to this succession of cascades the name "Crystal fall." It is very beautiful; but the broken and cavernous gorge through which it passes, worn into a thousand fantastic shapes, bearing along its margin the tracks of grizzly bears and lesser wild animals, scattered throughout with huge masses of obsidian and other volcanic matter—the whole suggestive of nothing earthly nor heavenly—received at our hands, and not inaptly as I conceive, the name of "The Devil's Den."

I presume that many persons will question the taste evinced by our company in the selection of names for the various objects of interest we have thus far met with; but they are all so different from any of Nature's works that we have ever seen or heard of, so entirely out of range of human experience, and withal so full of exhibitions which can suggest no other fancy than that which our good grandmothers have painted on our boyish imaginations as a destined future abode, that we are likely, almost involuntarily, to pursue the system with which we have commenced, to the end of our journey. A similar imagination has possessed travelers and visitors to other volcanic regions.

We have decided to remain at this point through the entire day to-morrow, and examine the cañon and falls. From the brief survey of the cañon I was enabled to make before darkness set in, I am impressed with its awful grandeur, and I realize the impossibility of giving to any one who has not seen a gorge similar in character, any idea of it.

It is getting late, and it is already past our usual bedtime, and Jake Smith is calling to me to "turn in" and give him a chance to sleep. There is in what I have already

Cornelius Hedges.

seen so much of novelty to fill the mind and burden the memory, that unless I write down in detail the events of each day, and indeed almost of each hour as it passes, I shall not be able to prepare for publication on my return home any clear or satisfactory account of these wonders. So Jake may go to. I will write until my candle burns out. Jacob is indolent and fond of slumber, and I think that he resents my remark to him the other day, that he could burn more and gather less wood than any man I ever camped with. He has dubbed me "The Yellowstone sharp." Good! I am not ashamed to have the title. Lieutenant Doane has crawled out of his blankets, and is just outside the tent with his hand and fore-arm immersed in water nearly as cold as ice. I am afraid that lock-jaw will set in if he does not consent to have the felon lanced.

Wednesday, August 31.—This has been a "red-letter" day with me, and one which I shall not soon forget, for my mind is clogged and my memory confused by what I have to-day seen. General Washburn and Mr. Hedges are sitting near me, writing, and we have an understanding that we will compare our notes when finished. We are all overwhelmed with astonishment and wonder at what we have seen, and we feel that we have been near the very presence of the Almighty. General Washburn has just quoted from the psalm:

"When I behold the work of Thy hands, what is man that Thou art mindful of him!"

My own mind is so confused that I hardly know where to commence in making a clear record of what is at this moment floating past my mental vision. I cannot confine myself to a bare description of the falls of the Yellowstone alone, for these two great cataracts are but one feature in a scene composed of so many of the elements of grandeur and sublimity, that I almost despair of giving to those who on our return home will listen to a recital of our ad-ventures, the faintest conception of it. The immense cañon or gorge of rocks through which the river descends, perhaps more than the falls, is calculated to fill the observer with feelings of mingled awe and terror. This chasm is seemingly about thirty miles in length. Commencing above the upper fall, it attains a depth of two hundred feet where that takes its plunge, and in the distance of half a mile from that point to the verge of the lower fall, it rapidly descends with the river between walls of rock nearly six hundred feet in vertical height, to which three hundred and twenty feet are added by the fall. Below this the wall lines marked by the descent of the river grow in height with incredible distinctness, until they are probably two thousand feet above the water. There is a difference of nearly three thousand feet in altitude between the surface of the river at the upper fall and the foot of the cañon. Opposite Mount Washburn the cañon must be more than half a vertical mile in depth. As it is impossible to explore the entire cañon, we are unable to tell whether the course of the river through it is broken by other and larger cataracts than the two we have seen, or whether its continuous descent alone has produced the enormous depth to which it has attained. Rumors of falls a thousand feet in height have often reached us before we made this visit. At all points where we approached the edge of the cañon the river was descending with fearful momentum through it, and the rapids and foam from the dizzy summit of the rock overhanging the lower fall, and especially from points farther down the cañon, were so terrible to behold, that none of our company could venture the experiment in any other manner than by lying prone upon the rock, to gaze into its awful depths; depths so amazing that the sound of the rapids in their course over immense boulders, and lashing in fury the base of the rocks on which we were lying, could not be heard. The stillness is horrible, and the solemn grandeur of the scene surpasses conception. You feel

GRAND CAÑON.

the absence of sound—the oppression of absolute silence. Down, down, down, you see the river attenuated to a thread. If you could only hear that gurgling river, lashing with puny strength the massive walls that imprison it and hold it in their dismal shadow, if you could but see a living thing in the depth beneath you, if a bird would but fly past you, if the wind would move any object in that awful chasm, to break for a moment the solemn silence which reigns there, it would relieve that tension of the nerves which the scene has excited, and with a grateful heart you would thank God that he had permitted you to gaze un-harmed upon this majestic display of his handiwork. But as it is, the spirit of man sympathizes with the deep gloom of the scene, and the brain reels as you gaze into this profound and solemn solitude.

The place where I obtained the best and most terrible view of the cañon was a narrow projecting point situated two or three miles below the lower fall.* Standing there or rather lying there for greater safety, I thought how ut-terly impossible it would be to describe to another the sen-sations inspired by such a presence. As I took in this scene, I realized my own littleness, my helplessness, my dread ex-posure to destruction, my inability to cope with or even comprehend the mighty architecture of nature. More than all this I felt as never before my entire dependence upon that Almighty Power who had wrought these wonders. A sense of danger, lest the rock should crumble away, almost overpowered me. My knees trembled, and I experienced the terror which causes men to turn pale and their counte-nances to blanch with fear, and I recoiled from the vision I had seen, glad to feel the solid earth beneath me and to realize the assurance of returning safety.

The scenery surrounding the cañon and falls on both banks of the Yellowstone is enlivened by all the hues of abundant vegetation. The foot-hills approach the river, crowned with a vesture of evergreen pines. Meadows ver-

*Now called Inspiration Point.

dant with grasses and shrubbery stretch away to the base
of the distant mountains, which, rolling into ridges, rising
into peaks, and breaking into chains, are defined in the
deepest blue upon the horizon. To render the scene still
more imposing, remarkable volcanic deposits, wonderful
boiling springs, jets of heated vapor, large collections of
sulphur, immense rocks and petrifications abound in great
profusion in this immediate vicinity. The river is filled
with trout, and bear, elk, deer, mountain lions and lesser
game roam the plains, forests and mountain fastnesses.

The two grand falls of the Yellowstone form a fitting
completion to this stupendous climax of wonders. They
impart life, power, light and majesty to an assemblage of
elements, which without them would be the most gloomy
and horrible solitude in nature. Their eternal anthem,
echoing from cañon, mountain, rock and woodland, thrills
you with delight, and you gaze with rapture at the iris-
crowned curtains of fleecy foam as they plunge into gulfs
enveloped in mist and spray. The stillness which held your
senses spellbound, as you peered into the dismal depths of
the cañon below, is now broken by the uproar of waters;
the terror it inspired is superseded by admiration and astonishment, and the scene, late so painful from its silence
and gloom, is now animate with joy and revelry.

The upper fall, as determined by the rude means of
measurement at our command, is one hundred and fifteen
feet in height. The river approaches it through a passage
of rocks which rise one hundred feet on either side above
its surface. Until within half a mile of the brink of the fall
the river is peaceful and unbroken by a ripple. Suddenly,
as if aware of impending danger, it becomes lashed into
foam, circled with eddies, and soon leaps into fearful rapids. The rocky jaws confining it gradually converge as it
approaches the edge of the fall, bending its course by

their projections, and apparently crowding back the
water, which struggles and leaps against their bases,
warring with its bounds in the impatience of restraint,
and madly leaping from its confines, a liquid emerald wreathed with foam, into the abyss beneath. The
sentinel rocks, a hundred feet asunder, could easily be
spanned by a bridge directly over and in front of the fall,
and fancy led me forward to no distant period when such
an effort of airy architecture would be crowded with happy
gazers from all portions of our country. A quarter of the
way between the verge and the base of the fall a rocky table projects from the west bank, in front of and almost
within reaching distance of it, furnishing a point of observation where the finest view can be obtained. In order
to get a more perfect view of the cararact, Mr. Hedges and
I made our way down to this table rock, where we sat for a
long time. As from this spot we looked up at the descending waters, we insensibly felt that the slightest protrusion
in them would hurl us backwards into the gulf below. A
thousand arrows of foam, apparently *aimed at us,* leaped
from the verge, and passed rapidly down the sheet. But as
the view grew upon us, and we comprehended the power,
majesty and beauty of the scene, we became insensible to
danger and gave ourselves up to the full enjoyment of it.

Very beautiful as is this fall, it is greatly excelled in
grandeur and magnificence by the cataract half a mile below it, where the river takes another perpendicular plunge
of three hundred and twenty feet into the most gloomy
cavern that ever received so majestic a visitant. Between
the two falls, the river, though bordered by lofty precipices,
expands in width and flows gently over a nearly level surface until its near approach to the verge. Here a sudden
convergence in the rocks compresses its channel, and with
a gurgling, choking struggle, it leaps with a single bound,

sheer from an even level shelf, into the tremendous chasm.
The sheet could not be more perfect if wrought by art.
The Almighty has vouchsafed no grander scene to human
eyes. Every object that meets the vision increases its sublimity. There is a majestic harmony in the whole, which

LOWER FALL OF THE YELLOWSTONE.

I have never seen before in nature's grandest works. The
fall itself takes its leap between the jaws of rocks whose
vertical height above it is more than six hundred feet, and
more than nine hundred feet above the chasm into which it
falls. Long before it reaches the base it is enveloped in

spray, which is woven by the sun's rays into bows radiant with all the colors of the prism, and arching the face of the cataract with their glories. Five hundred feet below the edge of the cañon, and one hundred and sixty feet above the verge of the cataract, and overlooking the deep gorge beneath, on the flattened summit of a projecting crag, I lay with my face turned into the boiling chasm, and with a stone suspended by a large cord measured its profoundest depths. Three times in its descent the cord was parted by abrasion, but at last, securing the weight with a leather band, I was enabled to ascertain by a measurement which I think quite exact, the height of the fall. It is a little more than three hundred and twenty feet; while the perpendicular wall down which I suspended the weight was five hundred and ten feet.

Looking down from this lofty eminence through the cañon below the falls, the scene is full of grandeur. The descent of the river for more than a mile is marked by continuous cascades varying in height from five to twenty feet, and huge rapids breaking over the rocks, and lashing with foam the precipitous sides of the gorge. A similar descent through the entire cañon (thirty miles), is probable, as in no other way except by distinct cataracts of enormous height can the difference in altitude between this point and its outlet be explained. The colors of the rock, which is shaly in character, are variegated with yellow, gray and brown, and the action of the water in its rapid passage down the sides of the cañon has worn the fragments of shale into countless capricious forms. Jets of steam issue from the sides of the cañon at frequent intervals, marking the presence of thermal springs and active volcanic forces. The evidence of a recession of the river through the cañon is designated by the ridges apparent on its sides, and it is not improbable that at no distant day the lower fall will become blended by this process with the upper, forming a single cataract nearly five hundred feet in height.

There are but few places where the sides of the Grand cañon can be descended with safety. Hauser and Stickney made the descent at a point where the river was 1,050 feet below the edge of the cañon, as determined by triangulation by Mr. Hauser. Lieutenant Doane, accompanied by his orderly, went down the river several miles, and following down the bed of a lateral stream reached its junction with the Yellowstone at a point where the cañon was about 1,500 feet in depth—the surface of the ground rising the farther he went down the river.

Mr. Hedges and I sat on the table-rock to which I have referred, opposite the upper fall, as long as our limited time would permit; and as we reluctantly left it and climbed to the top, I expressed my regret at leaving so fascinating a spot, quoting the familiar line:

"A thing of beauty is a joy forever."

Mr. Hedges asked me who was the author of the line, but I could not tell. I will look it up on my return.*

Yes! This stupendous display of nature's handiwork will be to me "a joy forever." It lingers in my memory like the faintly defined outlines of a dream. I can scarcely realize that in the unbroken solitude of this majestic range of rocks, away from civilization and almost inaccessible to human approach, the Almighty has placed so many of the most wonderful and magnificent objects of His creation, and that I am to be one of the few first to bring them to the notice of the world. Truly has it been said, that we live to learn how little may be known, and of what we see, how much surpasses comprehension.

*The above quotation is from a poem by John Keats.

Thursday, September 1.—We did not break camp till nearly ten o'clock this morning, the pack-train crossing Cascade creek at its head, and coming into the river trail about two miles above the upper fall. The more direct trail—shorter by one and a half miles—runs along the bank of the river.

If we had not decided, last night, that we would move on to-day, I think that every member of the party would have been glad to stay another day at the cañon and falls. I will, however, except out of the number our comrade Jake Smith. The afternoon of our arrival at the cañon (day before yesterday), after half an hour of inspection of the falls and cañon, he said: "Well, boys, I have seen all there is, and I am ready to move on."

However, the perceptible decline in our larder, and the uncertainty of the time to be occupied in further explorations, forbid more than these two days' stay at the falls and cañon. The sun this morning shone brightly, and its rays were reflected upon the sides of the dismal cañon—so dark, and gray, and still—enlivening and brightening it. To-day has been warm, and nature this morning seemed determined that our last look should be the brightest, for the beauties of the entire landscape invited us to make a longer stay, and we lingered till the last moment, that the final impression might not be lost.

Pursuing our journey, at two miles above the falls we crossed a small stream which we named "Alum" creek, as it is strongly impregnated with alum.

Six miles above the upper fall we entered upon a region remarkable for the number and variety of its hot springs and craters. The principal spring, and the one that first meets the eye as you approach from the north, is a hot sulphur spring, of oval shape, the water of which is constantly boiling and is thrown up to the height of from three to sev-

W. C. Gillette.

en feet. Its two diameters are about twelve feet and twenty feet, and it has an indented border of seemingly pure sulphur, about two feet wide and extending down into the spring or cauldron to the edge of the water, which at the time of our visit, if it had been at rest, would have been fifteen or eighteen inches below the rim of the spring. · This spring is situated at the base of a low mountain, and the gentle slope below and around the spring for the distance of two hundred or three hundred feet is covered to the depth of from three to ten inches with the sulphurous deposit from the overflow of the spring. The moistened bed of a dried-up rivulet, leading from the edge of the spring down inside through this deposit, showed us that the spring had but recently been overflowing. Farther along the base of this mountain is a sulphurous cavern about twenty feet deep, and seven or eight feet in diameter at its mouth, out of which the steam is thrown in jets with a sound resembling the puffing of a steam-boat when laboring over a sand-bar, and with as much uniformity and intonation as if emitted by a high-pressure engine. From hundreds of fissures in the adjoining mountain from base to summit, issue hot sulphur vapors, the apertures through which they escape being encased in thick incrustations of sulphur, which in many instances is perfectly pure. There are nearby a number of small sulphur springs, not especially remarkable in appearance.

About one hundred yards from these springs is a large hot spring of irregular shape, but averaging forty feet long by twenty-five wide, the water of which is of a dark muddy color. Still farther on are twenty or thirty springs of boiling mud of different degrees of consistency and color, and of sizes varying from two to eight feet in diameter, and of depths below the surface varying from three to eight feet. The mud in these springs is in most cases a little thinner

than mortar prepared for plastering, and, as it is thrown
up from one to two feet, I can liken its appearance to
nothing so much as Indian meal hasty pudding when
the process of boiling is nearly completed, except that the
puffing, bloated bubbles are greatly magnified, being from
a few inches to two feet in diameter. In some of the
springs the mud is of dark brown color, in others nearly
pink, and in one it was almost yellow. Springs four or five
feet in diameter and not over six feet apart, have no connection one with another either above or beneath the surface, the mud in them being of different colors. In some
instances there is a difference of three feet in the height to
which the mud in adjoining springs attains. There may
be in some instances two or more springs which receive
their supply of mud and their underground pressure from
the same general source, but these instances are rare, nor
can we determine positively that such is the case. This
mud having been worked over and over for many years is as
soft as the finest pigments.

All of these springs are embraced within a circle the
radius of which is from a thousand to twelve hundred feet,
and the whole of this surface seems to be a smothered
crater covered over with an incrustation of sufficient
strength and thickness to bear usually a very heavy weight,
but which in several instances yielded and even broke
through under the weight of our horses as we rode over it.
We quickly dismounted, and as we were making some examinations, the crust broke through several times in some
thin places through which vapor was issuing. Under the
whole of this incrustation the hottest fires seem to be
raging, and the heat issuing from the vents or from the
crevices caused from the breaking in of the surface is too
intense to be borne by the gloved hand for an instant.
Surrounding the natural vents are deposits of pure sul-

phur, portions of which in many instances we broke off, and after allowing them to cool, brought them away with us. On the top of the mountain overlooking the large sulphur spring is a small living crater about six inches in diameter, out of which issue hot vapor and smoke. On the slope adjoining the mud spring is another crater of irregular shape, but embracing about one hundred square inches, out of which issues hot vapor, the rocks adjoining changing color under the intense heat with every breath blown upon them.

The tramp of our horses' feet as we rode over the incrustation at the base of the mountain returned a hollow sound; yet while some of our party were not disposed to venture upon it with their horses, still I think with care in selecting a route there is very little danger in riding over it.

On the mountain, large quantities of sulphur formed by the condensation of the vapor issuing from the crevices, now closed, but once in activity in the incrusted covering, have been deposited, and we collected many specimens of pure and crystallized sulphur. Thousands of pounds of pure and nearly pure sulphur are now lying on the top and sides of the mountain, all of which can be easily gathered with the aid of a spade to detach it from the mountain side incrustations to which it adheres in the process of condensation. We gave to this mountain the name "Crater hill."

Five miles further on we camped near the "Mud geyser." Our course today has been for the greater part over a level valley, which was plainly visible from the top of Mount Washburn. The water of the river at this point is strongly impregnated with the mineral bases of the springs surrounding our camp, and that empty into the river above it.

Friday, September 2.—To-day we have occupied ourselves in examining the springs and other wonders at this point. At the base of the foot-hills adjoining our camp are three large springs of thick boiling mud, the largest of which resembles an immense cauldron. It is about thirty feet in diameter, bordered by a rim several feet wide, upon which one can stand within reach of the boiling mass of mud, the surface of which is four or five feet below the rim enclosing it, the rim being a little raised above the surrounding level. Some twelve or fifteen rods from this spring are two other springs from ten to twelve feet in diameter. Near by is a hot (not boiling) spring of sulphur, fifteen to eighteen feet in diameter, too hot to bathe in. From these we passed over the timbered hill at the base of which these springs are situated. In the timber along the brow of the hill and near its summit, and immediately under the living trees, the hot sulphur vapor and steam issue from several fissures or craters, showing that the hottest fires are raging at some point beneath the surface crust, which in a great many places gives forth a hollow sound as we pass over it. Through a little coulee on the other side of the hill runs a small stream of greenish water, which issues from a small cavern, the mouth of which is about five feet high and the same dimension in width. From the mouth, the roof of the cavern descends at an angle of about fifteen degrees, till at the distance of twenty feet from the entrance it joins the surface of the water. The bottom of the cavern under the water seems to descend at about the same angle, but as the water is in constant ebullition, we cannot determine this fact accurately. The water is thrown out in regular spasmodic jets, the pulsations occurring once in ten or twelve seconds. The sides and mouth of this cavern are covered with a dark green deposit, some of which we have taken with us for analysis. About two hundred yards farther on is another geyser, the flow of which occurs about every six hours, and when the crater is full the diameter of the surface is about fourteen feet, the sides of the crater being of an irregular funnel-shape, and descending at an angle of about forty-five degrees. At the lowest point at which we saw the water it was about seven feet in diameter on the surface. One or another of our party watched the gradual rise of the water for four or five hours. The boiling commenced when the water had risen half way to the surface, occasionally breaking forth with great violence. When the water had reached its full height in the basin, the stream was thrown up with great force to a height of from twenty to thirty feet, the column being from seven to ten feet in diameter at the midway height of the column, from bottom to top. The water was of a dark lead color, and those portions of the sides of the crater that were overflowed and then exposed by the rise and fall of the water were covered with stalagmites formed by the deposit from the geyser.

While surveying these wonders, our ears were constantly saluted by dull, thundering, booming sounds, resembling the reports of distant artillery. As we approached the spot whence they proceeded, the ground beneath us shook and trembled as from successive shocks of an earthquake. Ascending a small hillock, the cause of the uproar was found to be a mud volcano—the greatest marvel we have yet met with. It is about midway up a gentle pine-covered slope, above which on the lower side its crater, thirty feet in diameter, rises to a height of about thirty-five feet. Dense masses of steam issue with explosive force from this crater, into whose tapering mouth, as they are momentarily dispelled by the wind, we can see at a depth of about forty feet the regurgitating contents. The explosions are not uniform in force or time, varying from three to eight seconds, and occasionally with perfect regularity occurring every five seconds. They are very distinctly heard at the distance of half a mile, and the massive jets of vapor which accompany them burst forth like the smoke of burning gunpowder.

Some of these pulsations are much more violent than others, but each one is accompanied by the discharge of an immense volume of steam, which at once shuts off all view of the inside of the crater; but sometimes, during the few seconds intervening between the pulsations, or when a breeze for a moment carries the steam to one side of the crater, we can see to the depth of thirty feet into the volcano, but cannot often discover the boiling mud; though occasionally, when there occurs an unusually violent spasm or concussion, a mass of mud as large in bulk as a hogshead is thrown up as high as our heads, emitting blinding clouds of steam in all directions, and crowding all observers back from the edge of the crater. We were led to believe that this volcano has not been long in existence; but that it burst forth the present summer but a few months ago. The green leaves and the limbs of the surrounding forest trees are covered with fresh clay or mud, as is also the newly grown grass for the distance of 180 feet from the crater. On the top branches of some of the trees near by— trees 150 feet high—we found particles of dried mud that had fallen upon the high branches in their descent just after this first outburst, which must have thrown the contents of the volcano as high as 250 or 300 feet. Mr. Hauser, whose experience as an engineer and with projectile forces entitles his opinion to credit, estimates from the particles of mud upon the high trees, and the distance to which they were thrown, that the mud had been thrown, in this explosion, to the height of between 300 and 400 feet. By actual measurement we found particles of this mud 186 feet from the edge of the crater.

We did not dare to stand upon the leeward side of the crater and withstand the force of the steam; and Mr.

Hedges, having ventured too near the rim on that side, endangered his life by his temerity, and was thrown violently down the exterior side of the crater by the force of the volume of steam emitted during one of these fearful convulsions. General Washburn and I, who saw him fall, were greatly concerned lest while regaining his feet, being blinded by the steam, and not knowing in which direction to turn, he should fall into the crater.

Between the volcano, the mud geyser and the cavern spring are a number of hot sulphur and mud springs, of sizes varying from two to twenty feet in diameter, and many openings or crevices from which issue hot vapor or steam, the mouths of which are covered with sulphur deposits or other incrustations.

From the mud volcano we moved up the valley about four miles to our camp on the river, passing several mud puffs on the way. One of the soldiers brought in a large string of river trout, but the water of the river is strongly impregnated with the overflow from springs near its bank, and is not palatable. Some of our party who have drank the water are feeling nauseated. Others think that their illness is caused by partaking too freely of one of the luxuries of our larder, canned peaches. I assuaged my thirst with the peaches, and have not partaken of the water, and there is no one in our camp in finer condition than I am.

Lieutenant Doane's felon has caused him great suffering to-day, and I have appealed to him to allow me to lance it. I have for many years carried a lancet in my pocketbook, but I find that I have inadvertently left it at home. So all this day, while on horseback, I have been preparing for the surgical operation by sharpening my penknife on the leathern pommel of my saddle as I rode along. I have in my seamless sack a few simple medicines, including a vial of chloroform. Lieutenant Doane has almost agreed to let

me open the felon, provided I put him to sleep with the
chloroform; but I feel that I am too much of a novice in
the business to administer it. However, I have told him
that I would do so if he demanded it. Our elevation to-day
is about 7,500 feet above sea level.

Saturday, September 3.—This morning General Washburn and I left camp immediately after breakfast and returned four miles on our track of September 1st to Crater
Hill and the mud springs, for the purpose of making farther
examinations. We found the sulphur boiling spring to be
full to overflowing, the water running down the inclined
surface of the crust in two different directions. It was also
boiling with greater force than it was when we first saw it,
the water being occasionally thrown up to the height of ten
feet. About 80 or 100 yards from this spring we found
what we had not before discovered, a boiling spring of tar-
taric acid in solution, with deposits around the edge of the
spring, of which we gathered a considerable quantity. In
the basin where we had found so many mud springs we
to-day found a hot boiling spring containing a substance of
deep yellow color, the precise nature of which we could not
readily ascertain. We accordingly brought away some of
it in a bottle (as is our usual custom in such cases of uncertainty), and we will have an analysis of it made on our
return home. In the same basin we also found some specimens of black lava.

A half mile south of these springs we found an alum
spring yielding but little water and surrounded with beautiful alum crystals. From its border we obtained a great
many curiously shaped deposits of alum slightly impregnated with iron. The border of this spring below the surface had been undermined in many places by the violent
boiling of the water, to the distance of several feet from
the margin, so that it was unsafe to stand near the edge

of the spring.   This, however, I did not at first perceive; and, as I was unconcernedly passing by the spring, my weight made the border suddenly slough off beneath my feet. General Washburn noticed the sudden cracking of the incrustation before I did, and I was aroused to a sense of my peril by his shout of alarm, and had sufficient presence of mind to fall suddenly backwards at full length upon the sound crust, whence, with my feet and legs extended over the spring, I rolled to a place of safety.   But for General Washburn's shout of alarm, in another instant I would have been precipitated into this boiling pool of alum.   We endeavored to sound the depth of this spring with a pole twenty-five feet long, but we found no bottom.

Everything around us—air, earth, water—is impregnated with sulphur.   We feel it in every drop of water we drink, and in every breath of air we inhale.   Our silver watches have turned to the color of poor brass, tarnished.

General Washburn and I again visited the mud vulcano to-day.   I especially desired to see it again for the one especial purpose, among others of a general nature, of assuring myself that the notes made in my diary a few days ago are not exaggerated.   No! they are not!   The sensations inspired in me to-day, on again witnessing its convulsions, and the dense clouds of vapor expelled in rapid succession from its crater, amid the jarring of the earth, and the ominous intonations from beneath, were those of mingled dread and wonder.   At war with all former experience it was so novel, so unnaturally natural, that I feel while now writing and thinking of it, as if my own senses might have deceived me with a mere figment of the imagination.   But it is not so.   The wonder, than which this continent, teeming with nature's grandest exhibitions, contains nothing more marvelous, still stands amid the solitary fastnesses of the Yellowstone, to excite the astonishment of the thousands who in coming years shall visit that remarkable locality.*

Returning to the camp we had left in the morning, we found the train had crossed the river, and we forded at the same place, visiting, however, on our way another large cauldron of boiling mud lying nearly opposite our camp. Soon after fording the river we discovered some evidence that trappers had long ago visited this region. Here we found that the earth had been thrown up two feet high, presenting an angle to the river, quite ingeniously concealed by willows, and forming a sort of rifle-pit, from which a

---

*Dr. F. V. Hayden, geologist in charge of the U. S. Geological Survey, first visited this region in the summer of 1871—the year following the visit of the Washburn party, whose discoveries and explorations are recorded in this diary. Dr. Hayden, on his return, graphically described the various wonders which he saw, but had very little to say concerning the mud volcano. This fact was the more inexplicable to me for the reason that the Washburn party thought it one of the most remarkable curiosities to be found in that region, and I was greatly surprised to find that Dr. Hayden made so little allusion to it.

In 1872, the year following Dr. Hayden's first visit, I again visited the volcano, and the omission by Hayden was explained as soon as I saw the volcano in its changed condition. The loud detonations which resembled the discharges of a gun-boat mortar were no longer heard, and the upper part of the crater and cone had in a great measure disappeared, leaving a shapeless and unsightly hole much larger than the former crater, in which large tree-tops were swaying to and fro in the gurgling mass, forty feet below—the whole appearance bearing testimony to the terrible nature of the convulsion which wrought such destruction. Lieutenant Doane, in his official report to the War Department, thus describes the volcano as it appeared in 1870:

"A few hundred yards from here is an object of the greatest interest. On the slope of a small and steep wooded ravine is the crater of a mud volcano, 30 feet in diameter at the rim, which is elevated a few feet above the surface on the lower side, and bounded by the slope of the hill on the upper, converging, as it deepens, to the diameter of 15 feet at the lowest visible point, about 40 feet down. Heavy volumes of steam escape from this opening, ascending to the height of 300 feet. From far down in the earth came a jarring sound, in regular beats of five seconds, with a concussion that shook the ground at 200 yards' distance. After each concussion came a splash of mud, as if thrown to a great height;

hunter without disclosing his hiding place could bring down swans, geese, ducks, pelicans, and even the furred animals that made their homes along the river bank.

We followed the trail of the advance party along the bank of the river, and most of the way through a dense forest of pine timber and over a broad swampy lowland, when we came into their camp on the Yellowstone lake two miles from where it empties into the river, and about ten miles from our morning camp. We passed Brimstone basin on our left, and saw jets of steam rising from the hills back of it. From all appearances the Yellowstone can be forded

---

sometimes it could be seen from the edge of the crater, but none was entirely ejected while we were there. Occasionally an explosion was heard like the bursting of heavy guns behind an embankment, and causing the earth to tremble for a mile around. The distance to which this mud had been thrown is truly astonishing. The ground and falling trees near by were splashed at a horizontal distance of 200 feet. The trees below were either broken down or their branches festooned with dry mud, which appeared in the tops of the trees growing on the side hill from the same level with the crater, 50 feet in height, and at a distance of 180 feet from the volcano. The mud, to produce such effects, must have been thrown to a perpendicular elevation of at least 300 feet. It was with difficulty we could believe the evidence of our senses, and only after the most careful measurements could we realize the immensity of this wonderful phenomenon."

The visitor to the Park who has read the description given by Washburn, Hedges, Doane or myself, of the mud volcano as it appeared in 1870, will readily perceive that it has undergone a great change since the time of its first discovery.

In my account of my trip made in 1872, published in Scribner's (now Century) Magazine for June, 1873, I say, concerning this change: "A large excavation remained; and a seething, bubbling mass of mud, with several tree-tops swaying to and fro in the midst, told how terrible and how effectual must have been the explosions which produced such devastation. I could not realize that in this unsightly hole I beheld all that was left of those physical wonders which filled this extraordinary region. * * * Great trees that then decorated the hillside were now completely submerged in the boiling mass that remained."

The trees with their green tops, which were visible in 1872, have now entirely disappeared. Can any one conjecture what has become of them?

at almost any point between the rapids just above the upper fall and the lake, unless there are quicksands and crevices which must be avoided.

Yellowstone lake, as seen from our camp to-night, seems to me to be the most beautiful body of water in the world. In front of our camp it has a wide sandy beach like that of the ocean, which extends for miles and as far as the eye can reach, save that occasionally there is to be found a sharp projection of rocks. The overlooking bench rises from the water's edge about eight feet, forming a bank of sand or natural levee, which serves to prevent the overflow of the land adjoining, which, when the lake is receiving the water from the mountain streams that empty into it while the snows are melting, is several feet below the surface of the lake. On the shore of the lake, within three or four miles of our camp, are to be found specimens of sandstone, resembling clay, of sizes varying from that of a walnut to a flour barrel, and of every odd shape imaginable. Fire and water have been at work here together—fire to throw out the deposit in a rough shape, and water to polish it. From our camp we can see several islands from five to ten miles distant in a direct line. Two of the three "Tetons," which are so plainly visible to travelers going to Montana from Eagle Rock bridge on Snake river, and which are such well-known and prominent landmarks on that stage route, we notice to-night in the direction of south 25 degrees west from our camp. We shall be nearer to them on our journey around the lake.

Sunday, September 4.—This morning at breakfast time Lieutenant Doane was sleeping soundly and snoring sonorously, and we decided that we would not waken him, but would remain in camp till the afternoon and perhaps until morning. Walter Trumbull suggested that a proper deference to Jake Smith's religious sentiments ought to be a sufficient reason for not traveling on Sunday, whereupon Jake immediately exclaimed, "If we're going to remain in camp, let's have a game of draw."

Last evening Lieutenant Doane's sufferings were so intense that General Washburn and I insisted that he submit to an operation, and have the felon opened, and he consented provided I would administer chloroform. Preparations were accordingly made after supper. A box containing army cartridges was improvised as an operating table, and I engaged Mr. Bean, one of our packers, and Mr. Hedges as assistant surgeons. Hedges was to take his position at Doane's elbow, and was to watch my motion as I thrust in the knife blade, and hold the elbow and fore-arm firmly to prevent any involuntary drawing back of the arm by Lieutenant Doane, at the critical moment. When Doane was told that we were ready, he asked, "Where is the chloroform?" I replied that I had never administered it, and that after thinking the matter over I was afraid to assume the responsibility of giving it. He swallowed his disappointment, and turned his thumb over on the cartridge box, with the nail down. Hedges and Bean were on hand to steady the arm, and before one could say "Jack Robinson," I had inserted the point of my penknife, thrusting it down to the bone, and had ripped it out to the end of the thumb. Doane gave one shriek as the released corruption flew out in all directions upon surgeon and assistants, and then with a broad smile on his face he exclaimed, "That was elegant!" We then applied a poultice of bread and water, which we renewed a half hour later, and Doane at about eight o'clock last night dropped off into a seemingly peaceful sleep, which has been continuous up to the time of this writing, two o'clock p. m.*

---

*Lieutenant Doane, on page 19 of his report to the War Department, says with reference to this surgical operation:

Evening of September 4.—I have been glad to have this
rest to-day, for with the time spent in writing up a detailed diary in addition to the work about camp, I have
been putting in about sixteen hours work each day.   So
this afternoon a nap of two or three hours was a pleasant
rest.   I strolled for a long distance down the shore, the
sand of which abounds in small crystals, which some of
our party think may possess some value.   Craters emitting
steam through the water are frequently seen beneath the
surface, at a distance of from forty to fifty feet from its
margin, the water in which is very hot, while that of the
lake surrounding them I found to be too cool for a pleasant
bath.   In some places the lake water is strongly impregnated with sulphur.   One crater emits a jet of steam with
a hissing noise as loud as that usually heard at the blow-
ing off of the safety valve of a steamboat.   In the clear
light of the setting sun, we can see the three Tetons in a
southwesterly direction.

Some member of our party has asked what is the meaning
of the word "Teton" given to these mountains.*   Lieutenant

"I had on the previous evening been nine days and nights without sleep or rest, and was becoming very much reduced.   My hand
was enormously swelled, and even ice water ceased to relieve the
pain.   I could scarcely walk at all, from excessive weakness.   The
most powerful opiates had ceased to have any effect.   A consultation was held, which resulted in having the thumb split open.   Mr.
Langford performed the operation in a masterly manner, dividing
thumb, bone, and all.   An explosion ensued, followed by immediate
relief.   I slept through the night, all day, and the next night, and
felt much better.   To Mr. Langford, General Washburn, Mr. Stickney and the others of the party I owe a lasting debt for their uniform kindness and attention in the hour of need."

*Repeated efforts to ascend the Grand Teton, made prior to the
year 1872, all terminated in failure.   On the 29th day of July of that
year the summit was reached by James Stevenson, of the U. S. Geological Survey, and Nathaniel P. Langford, the writer of this diary.
An account of this ascent was published in Scribner's (now Century) Magazine for June, 1873.   The next ascent was made in 1898
by Rev. Frank S. Spalding, of Erie, Pennsylvania, and W. O. Owen,

The Grand Teton, Wyoming.
13762 feet high.

The saddle
about 2500 feet
below the Summit.

GRAND TETON.

Doane says it is a French word signifying "Woman's Breast," and that it was given to these mountains by the early French explorers, because of their peculiar shape. I think that the man who gave them this name must have seen them from a great distance; for as we approach them, the graceful curvilinear lines which obtained for them this delicate appellation appear angular and ragged. From our present point of view the name seems a misnomer. If there were twelve of them instead of three, they might better be called the "Titans," to illustrate their relation to the surrounding country. He indeed must have been of a most susceptible natur'e, and, I would fain believe, long a dweller amid these solitudes, who could trace in these cold and barren peaks any resemblance to the gentle bosom of woman.

Monday, September 5.—Lieutenant Doane continued to sleep all last night, making a thirty-six hours nap, and after dressing his thumb and taking an observation to determine our elevation, which we found to be 7714 feet above the ocean, we broke camp at nine o'clock. After the train had got under way, I asked Mr. Hedges to remain behind and assist me in measuring, by a rude system of triangulation, the distance across the lake as well as to the Tetons; but owing to the difficulty we encountered in laying out a base line of sufficient length, we abandoned the scheme after some two hours of useless labor.

---

of Wyoming, and two assistants. This ascent was accomplished after two failures of Mr. Owen in previous years to reach the summit. Mr. Owen then asserted that the summit of the mountain was not reached in 1872 by Stevenson and Langford. His efforts—in which Mr. Spalding had no part—to impeach the statement of these gentlemen failed utterly. Mr. Spalding, who was the first member of his party to reach the summit, writes: "I believe that Mr. Langford reached the summit because he says he did, and because the difficulties of the ascent were not great enough to have prevented any good climber from having successfully scaled the peak, * * * and I cannot understand why Mr. Owen failed so many times before he succeeded."

Following the trail of the advance party, we traveled along the lake beach for about six miles, passing a number of small hot sulphur springs and lukewarm sulphur ponds, and three hot steam jets surrounded by sulphur incrustations. After six miles, we left the beach, and traveled on the plateau overlooking the lake. This plateau was covered with a luxuriant growth of standing pine and a great deal of fallen timber, through which at times considerable

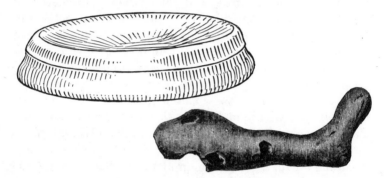

SLATE SPECIMENS FROM CURIOSITY POINT.
SLATE CUP.   LEG AND FOOT.

difficulty was experienced in passing. A little way from the trail is an alkaline spring about six feet in diameter. We came to camp on the shore of the lake, after having marched fifteen miles in a southerly direction. We have a most beautiful view of the lake from our camp. Yesterday it lay before us calm and unruffled, save by the waves which gently broke upon the shore. To-day the winds lash it into a raging sea, covering its surface with foam, while the sparkling sand along the shore seems to form for it a jeweled setting, and the long promontories stretching out into it, with their dense covering of pines, lend a charming feature to the scene. Water never seemed so beautiful before. Waves four feet high are rolling in, and there appear to be six or seven large islands; but we cannot be certain about this number until we reach the south shore. From this point we cannot tell whether the wooded hills before us are islands or promontories. On the shore are to be found large numbers of carnelians or crystallized quartz, agates, specimens of petrified wood, and lava pebbles or globules. We have found also many curious objects of slate formation, resembling hollowed-out cups, discs, and two well formed resemblances of a leg and foot, and many other curious objects which Nature in her most capricious mood has scattered over this watery solitude. All these seem to be the joint production of fire and water; the fire forming and baking them, and the water polishing them. We called this place "Curiosity Point."

If Mount Washington were set in the lake, its summit would be two thousand feet below the surface of the water.

To-night a conference of the party was held, to decide whether we would continue our journey around the lake, or retrace our steps and pass along the north side of the lake over to the Madison. By a vote of six to three we have decided to go around the lake. Mr. Hauser voted in favor of returning by way of the north side. My vote was cast for going around the lake.

As we passed along the shore to-day, we could see the steam rising from a large group of hot springs on the opposite shore of the lake bordering on what seems to be the most westerly bay or estuary.* We will have an opportunity to examine them at short range, when we have completed our journey around the lake.

---

*The bay here referred to is at the "Thumb" Station.

Tuesday, September 6.—We broke camp at ten thirty this morning, bearing well to the south-east for an hour and then turning nearly due south, our trail running through the woods, and for a large part of our route throughout the day, through fallen timber, which greatly impeded our progress. We did not make over ten miles in our day's travel. Frequently we were obliged to leave the trail running through the woods, and return to the lake, and follow the beach for some distance. We passed along the base of a brimstone basin, the mountains forming a semi-circle half way around it, the lake completing the circle. In company with Lieutenant Doane I went up the side of the mountain, which for the distance of three or four miles and about half way to the summit is covered with what appears to be sulphate (?) of lime and flowers of sulphur mixed. Exhalations are rising from all parts of the ground at times, the odor of brimstone being quite strong; but the volcanic action in this vicinity is evidently decreasing.

About half way up the deposit on the mountain side a number of small rivulets take their rise, having sulphur in solution, and farther down the mountain and near the base are the dry beds of several streams from ten to twenty feet in width which bear evidence of having at some time been full to the banks (two or three feet deep) with sulphur water. The small streams now running are warm.

The side of the mountain over which we rode, seems for the most part to be hollow, giving forth a rumbling sound beneath the feet, as we rode upon the crust, which is very strong. In no instance did it give way as did the crust at "Crater hill," under which the fires were raging, though the incrustation appears to be very similar, abounding in vents and fissures and emitting suffocating exhalations of sulphur vapor.

On the sides of the mountain were old fissures, surrounded by rusty looking sulphur incrustations, now nearly washed away. The whole mountain gives evidence of having been, a long time ago, in just the same condition of conflagration as that in which we found "Crater hill;" but all outward trace of fire has now disappeared, save what is found in the warm water of the small streams running down the sides.

Our course for the past two days has been in nearly a south-southeast direction, or about parallel with the Wind river mountains. We have today seen an abundance of the tracks of elk and bears, and occasionally the track of a mountain lion.

Wednesday, September 7.—Last night when all but the guards were asleep, we were startled by a mountain lion's shrill scream, sounding so like the human voice that for a moment I was deceived by it into believing that some traveler in distress was hailing our camp. The stream near the bank of which our camp lay, flows into the southeast arm of Yellowstone lake, and for which the name "Upper Yellowstone" has been suggested by some of our party; but Lieutenant Doane says that he thinks he has seen on an old map the name "Bridger" given to some body of water near the Yellowstone. We tried to cross the river near its mouth, but found the mud in the bed of the stream and in the bottom lands adjoining too deep; our horses miring down to their bellies. In accordance with plans agreed upon last night, General Washburn and a few of the party started out this morning in advance of the others to search for a practicable crossing of the river and marshes, leaving the pack train in camp.

In company with Lieutenant Doane I went out upon a reconnaissance for the purpose of determining the elevation of the mountains opposite our camp, as well as the

shape of the lake as far as we could see the shore, and also
to determine as far as possible our locality and the best
line of travel to follow in passing around the lake.   There
is just enough excitement attending these scouting expeditions to make them a real pleasure, overbalancing the labor
attendant upon them.   There is very little probability that
any large band of Indians will be met with on this side of
the lake, owing to the superstitions which originate in the
volcanic forces here found.

We followed along the high bank adjacent to the bottom
through which the river runs in a direction a little south
of east for the distance of about three miles, when we entered a heavily timbered ravine, which we followed through
the underbrush for some three miles, being frequently
obliged to dismount and lead our horses over the projecting
rocks, or plunging through bushes and fallen timber.   At
the end of two hours we reached a point in the ascent
where we could no longer ride in safety, nor could our
horses climb the mountain side with the weight of our bod-
ies on their backs.   Dismounting, we took the bridle reins
in our hands, and for the space of an hour we led our horses
up the steep mountain side, when we again mounted and
slowly climbed on our way, occasionally stopping to give
our horses a chance to breathe.   Arriving at the limit of
timber and of vegetation, we tied our horses, and then commenced the ascent of the steepest part of the mountain,
over the broken granite, great care being necessary to avoid
sliding down the mountain side with the loose granite.
The ascent occupied us a little more than four hours, and
all along the mountain side, even to near the summit, we
saw the tracks of mountain sheep.   The view from the summit of this mountain, for wild and rugged grandeur, is surpassed by none I ever before saw.   The Yellowstone basin
and the Wind river mountains were spread out before us

like a map. On the south the eye followed the source of
the Yellowstone above the lake, until, twenty-five miles
away, it was lost in an immense cañon, beyond which two
immense jets of vapor rose to a height of probably three
hundred feet, indicating that there were other and perhaps
greater wonders than those embraced in our prescribed
limit of exploration. On the north the outlet of the lake
and the steam from the mud geyser and mud volcano were
distinctly visible, while on the southeast the view followed
to the horizon a succession of lofty peaks and ridges at least
thirty miles in width, whose jagged slopes were filled with
yawning caverns, pine-embowered recesses and beetling
precipices, some hundreds and some thousands of feet in
height. This is the range which Captain Raynolds, ap-
proaching from the east, found impassable while on his exploring tour to the Yellowstone in the year 1860. I shall,
upon my return home, read Captain Raynolds' report with
renewed interest.*

The mountain on which we stood was the most westerly
peak of a range which, in long extended volume, swept to
the southeastern horizon, exhibiting a continuous elevation

---

*Captain Raynolds wrote on May 10, 1860: "To our front and
upon the right the mountains towered above us to the height of
from 2,000 to 3,000 feet in the shape of bold, craggy peaks of
basaltic formation, their summits crowned with glistening snow.
* * * * It was my original desire to go from the head of Wind
river to the head of the Yellowstone, keeping on the Atlantic slope,
thence down the Yellowstone, passing the lake ,and across by the
Gallatin to the Three forks of the Missouri. Bridger said, at the
outset, that this would be impossible, and that it would be necessary to pass over to the head waters of the Columbia, and back
again to the Yellowstone. I had not previously believed that crossing the main crest twice would be more easily accomplished than
the travel over what in effect is only a spur; but the view from our
present camp settled the question adversely to my opinion at once.
Directly across our route lies a basaltic ridge, rising not less than
5,000 feet above us, the walls apparently vertical, with no visible
pass nor even cañon. On the opposite side of this are the head
waters of the Yellowstone."

more than thirty miles in width, its central line broken into countless points, knobs, glens and defiles, all on the most colossal scale of grandeur and magnificence. Outside of these, on either border, along the entire range, lofty peaks rose at intervals, seemingly vying with each other in the varied splendors they presented to the beholder. The scene was full of majesty. The valley at the base of this range was dotted with small lakes. Lakes abound everywhere—in the valleys, on the mountains and farther down on their slopes, at all elevations. The appearance of the whole range was suggestive of the existence, ages since, of a high plateau on a level with these peaks (which seemed to be all of the same elevation), which by the action of the water had been cut down in the intervals between the peaks into deep gorges and cañons. The sides of the mountains formed in many places a perpendicular wall from 600 to 1,000 feet in height.

This range of mountains has a marvelous history. As it is the loftiest, so it is probably the most remarkable lateral ridge of the Rocky range. In the expedition sent across the continent by Mr. Astor, in 1811, under command of Captain Wilson P. Hunt, that gentleman met with the first serious obstacle to his progress at the eastern base of this range. After numerous efforts to scale it, he turned away and followed the valley of Snake river, encountering the most discouraging disasters until he arrived at Astoria.*

I have read somewhere (I think in Washington Irving's "Astoria" or "Bonneville's Adventures") that the Indians

---

*Later, in 1833, the indomitable Captain Bonneville was lost in this mountain labyrinth, and, after devising various modes of escape, finally determined to ascend the range.

Washington Irving, in his charming history, "Bonneville's Adventures," thus describes the efforts of General Bonneville and one of his comrades to reach the summit of this range:

"After much toil he reached the summit of a lofty cliff, but it was only to behold gigantic peaks rising all around, and towering far into the snowy regions of the atmosphere. He soon found that

regard this ridge of mountains as the crest of the world, and that among the Blackfeet there is a fable that he who attains its summit catches a view of the "Land of Souls" and beholds the "Happy Hunting Grounds" spread out be-low him, brightening with the abodes of the free and gen-erous spirits.

Lieutenant Doane and I were somewhat fatigued with our climb of four hours' duration, and we refreshed our-selves with such creature comforts as we found on the sum-mit; but, although we attained the "crest," we did not dis-cern any "free and generous spirit," save that which we saw "through a glass darkly."

At the point where we left our horses there was, on the east slope of the mountain, a body of snow, the surface of which was nearly horizontal, and the outer edge of which was thirty feet in perpendicular height. This body of snow is perpetual. At this point the elevation, as indicated by our aneroid barometer, was 9,476 feet, while at the summit it was 10,327 feet, a difference of 581 feet, which was the broken granite summit.

The descent occupied an hour and a quarter, when we struck the trail of the pack train near the base of the mountain, which we followed until we found three poles placed in the form of a tripod, the longer pole pointing to

---

he had undertaken a tremendous task; but the pride of man is never more obstinate than when climbing mountains. The ascent was so steep and rugged that he and his companion were frequently obliged to clamber on hands and knees, with their guns slung upon their backs. Frequently, exhausted with fatigue and dripping with perspiration, they threw themselves upon the snow, and took hand-fuls of it to allay their parching thirst. At one place they even stripped off their coats and hung them upon the bushes, and thus lightly clad proceeded to scramble over these eternal snows. As they ascended still higher there were cool breezes that refreshed and braced them, and, springing with new ardor to their task, they at length attained the summit."

the right to indicate that at this point the party had changed its course.

Obeying this Indian sign, we descended the bank border-ing the valley and traversed the bottom lands to the river, which we forded at a point where it was about ninety feet wide and three feet deep, with a current of about six miles an hour. This was about six or seven miles from the mouth of the river. We followed the trail of the advance party through a beautiful pine forest, free from underbrush, for the distance of two miles, passing two beautiful lakes. By this time night had overtaken us, and it was with difficulty that we could follow the trail, the tracks of the horses' shoes, which were our sole guide, being hardly discernible. But we pressed on, following the dark, serpentine line of freshly disturbed earth till it turned up the side of the mountain, where we followed it for upwards of a mile. Fearing lest we were not upon the right trail, we dismount-ed, and, placing our faces close to the ground, examined it carefully, but could not discover the impression of a single horseshoe. Gathering a few dry branches of pine, we kin-dled a fire upon the trail, when we discovered that we had been following, from the base of the mountain, the trail of a band of elk that had crossed the line of travel of the pack train at a point near the base of the mountain, and in the dim twilight we had not discovered the mistake.

The prospect for a night on the mountain, without blankets or supper, seemed now very good; but we retraced our

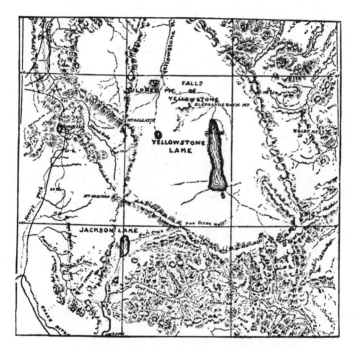

MAP OF YELLOWSTONE LAKE,
As known between 1860 and 1870.
From the map of
Raynolds' Expedition of 1860.

steps as rapidly as possible, and on reaching the base of the mountain, struck out for the lake, resolving to follow the beach, trusting that our party had made their camp on

MAP OF YELLOWSTONE LAKE.
Copy of
THE ORIGINAL OUTLINE SKETCHED BY
NATHANIEL P. LANGFORD
FROM THE TOP OF MOUNT LANGFORD, SEPT. 7, 1870,
AND COMPLETED SEPT. 10 AND 13.

the shore of the lake, in which case we should find them; but if camped at any considerable distance from the shore, we should not find them. Our ride over fallen timber and through morass for the distance of about two miles to the shore of the lake was probably performed more skillfully in the darkness of the night than if we had seen the obstacles in our path, and as we rounded a point on the smooth beach we saw at a distance of a little over a mile the welcome watch fire of our comrades. When we arrived within hailing distance we gave a loud halloo, and the ready response by a dozen sympathetic voices of our companions-in-arms showed that our own anxiety had been shared by them. Our camp to-night is on the westerly side of the most southeasterly bay of the lake. These bays are separated by long points of land extending far out into the lake. From our camp of two days ago some of these points seemed to be islands. From the top of the mountain, which Doane and I ascended to-day, I made an outline map of the north and east sides of the lake and part of the south side; but on account of the heavy timber on the promontories I could not make a correct outline of the south and west shores. General Washburn and Hauser, as well as myself, have thus far made outlines of the lake shore as best we could from points on a level with the lake, but these have been unsatisfactory and have lacked completeness, and Washburn and Hauser have both expressed their satisfaction with the sketch of the lake shore I made to-day from the top of the mountain; and Washburn has just told me that Lieutenant Doane has suggested that, as I was the first to reach the summit of the mountain, the peak should be named for me. I shall be gratified if this is done.*

---

*Soon after the return of our party to Helena, General Washburn, then surveyor-general of Montana, made in his office for the Interior Department at Washington, a map of the Yellowstone

We have traveled from our morning camp about twelve miles, but we are not more than four miles from it in a straight line.

Thursday, September 8.—Travel to-day has led us in zig-zag directions over fallen timber some twelve miles. We have halted on a small creek about one mile from the most southerly arm of the lake and about seven miles in a straight line from our morning camp.

This has been a terrible day for both men and horses. The standing trees are so thick that we often found it impossible

region, a copy of which he gave to me. He told me that in recognition of the assistance I had rendered him in making a fair outline of Yellowstone lake, with its indented shore and promontories, he had named for me the mountain on the top of which I stood when I made the sketch of the south shore of the lake. I called his attention to the fact that Lieutenant Doane had been my comrade in making the ascent, and suggested that Doane's name be given to the adjoining peak on the north. He approved of this suggestion, and the map, with these mountains so named, was transmitted to the Interior Department.

Dr. Hayden, the geologist in charge of the United States geological survey, made his first visit to this region the following year (1871), and on the map which he issued in connection with his 1871 report, the name "Mount Langford" was given to another mountain far to the northeast. Since that time my name has again been transferred to a mountain on the southeast. I think that Dr. Hayden must have been aware at that time that this mountain bore my name; for he had read the account of the Washburn exploration, which was published in Scribner's Magazine for May, 1871, accompanied by a copy of the map made by General Washburn.

The significance of connecting my name with this mountain is centered in the circumstance that it was intended to mark or commemorate an important event—that of giving to the public a very correct outline map of Yellowstone lake. In confirmation of the fact that the first outline of the lake approximating any degree of accuracy was made from the mountain-top, I here quote from page 21 of Lieutenant Doane's report to the War Department.

"The view from this peak commanded completely the lake, enabling us to sketch a map of its inlets and bearings with considerable accuracy."

On page 23 of this report Lieutenant Doane speaks of this mountain as "Mount Langford." The map last published previous to that made by General Washburn was that of Captain Raynolds, of which I here present a copy, as well as a copy of the map made by me.

to find a space wide enough for the pack animals to squeeze through, and we were frequently separated from each other in a search for a route. Hedges and Stickney, in this way, became separated from the rest of the party, and after suffering all the feelings of desolation at being lost in this wilderness, accidentally stumbled upon our camp, and they freely expressed their joy at their good fortune in being restored to the party. I fully sympathized with them, for, speaking from a personal experience of a similar character which I had in 1862, I can say that a man can have no more complete sense of utter desolation than that which overwhelms him when he realizes that he is lost.

At one point while they were seeking some sign of the trail made by the rest of the party, a huge grizzly bear dashed by them, frightening Hedges' horse, which broke his bridle and ran away.

After supper Washburn and Hauser went up on the ridge back of the camp to reconnoiter and ran across a she grizzly and her two cubs. Being unarmed, they hastily returned to camp for their guns, and five or six of us joined them in a bear hunt. The members of this hunting party were all elated at the thought of bagging a fine grizzly, which seemed an easy prey. What could one grizzly do against six hunters when her instinctive duty would lead her to hurry her little ones to a place of safety!

While putting our guns in order and making other preparations for the attack, an animated discussion took place concerning a proper disposition of the two cubs which were to be captured alive. Some of our party thought that they ought to be carried home to Helena, but Bean and Reynolds, our packers, being appealed to, thought the plan not feasible unless they could be utilized as pack animals. When we reached the spot where Washburn and Hauser had last seen the bear, we traced her into a dense thicket, which, owing to the darkness, we did not care to penetrate, for not one of us felt that we had lost that particular bear. Jake Smith, with more of good sense than usual, but with his usual lack of scriptural accuracy, remarked, "I always considered Daniel a great fool to go into a den of bears."*

Our journey for the entire day has been most trying, leading us through a trackless forest of pines encumbered on all sides by prostrate trunks of trees. The difficulty of urging forward our pack train, making choice of routes, extricating the horses when wedged between the trees, and re-adjusting the packs so that they would not project beyond the

---

*On our return to Helena, Walter Trumbull published, in the Helena Gazette, some incidents of our trip, and from his narrative I copy the following account of our hunt for the grizzly:

"Some of the party who had gone a short distance ahead to find out the best course to take the next day, soon returned and reported a grizzly and her two cubs about a quarter of a mile from camp. Six of the party decorated themselves as walking armories, and at once started in pursuit. Each individual was sandwiched between two revolvers and a knife, was supported around the middle by a belt of cartridges, and carried in his hand a needle carbine. Each one was particularly anxious to be the first to catch the bear, and an exciting foot-race ensued until the party got within 300 yards of the place where the bear was supposed to be concealed. The foremost man then suddenly got out of breath, and, in fact, they all got out of breath. It was an epidemic. A halt was made, and the brute loudly dared to come out and show itself, while a spirited discussion took place as to what was best to do with the cubs. The location was a mountain side, thickly timbered with tall straight pines having no limbs within thirty feet of the ground. It was decided to advance more cautiously to avoid frightening the animal, and every tree which there was any chance of climbing was watched with religious care, in order to intercept her should she attempt to take refuge in its branches. An hour was passed in vain search for the sneaking beast, which had evidently taken to flight. Then this formidable war party returned to camp, having a big disgust at the cowardly conduct of the bear, but, as the darkie said, 'not having it bad.' Just before getting in sight of camp, the six invincibles discharged their firearms simultaneously, in order to show those remaining behind just how they would have slaughtered the bear, but more particularly just how they did not. This was called the 'Bear Camp.' "

Mr. Trumbull was one of the party of hunters whose efforts to capture the bear he so well describes.

Benj. Stickney

sides of the horses, required constant patience and untiring toil, and the struggle between our own docility and the obstacles in our way, not unfrequently resulted in fits of sullenness or explosions of wrath which bore no slight resemblance to the volcanic forces of the country itself.

On one of these occasions when we were in a vast net of down timber and brush, and each man was insisting upon his own particular mode of extrication, and when our tempers had been sorely tried and we were in the most unsocial of humors, speaking only in half angry expletives, I recalled that beautiful line in Byron's "Childe Harold," "There is a pleasure in the pathless woods," which I recited with all the "ore rotundo" I could command, which struck the ludicrous vein of the company and produced an instantaneous response of uproarious laughter, which, so sudden is the transition between extremes, had the effect to restore harmony and sociability, and, in fact, to create a pleasure in the pathless wilderness we were traveling.

One of our pack horses is at once a source of anxiety and amusement to us all.   He is a remarkable animal owned by Judge Hedges, who, however, makes no pretentions to being a good judge of horses.   Mr. Hedges says that the man from whom he purchased the animal, in descanting upon his many excellent qualities, said: "He is that kind of an animal that drives the whole herd before him."   The man spoke truly, but Mr. Hedges did not properly interpret the encomium, nor did he realize that the seller meant to declare that the animal, from sheer exhaustion, would always be lagging behind the others of the herd.   From the start, and especially during our journey through the forest, this pony, by his acrobatic performances and mishaps, has furnished much amusement for us all.   Progress to-day could only be accomplished by leaping our animals over the fallen trunks of trees.   Our little broncho, with all the

spirit necessary, lacks oftentimes the power to scale the
tree trunks.   As a consequence, he is frequently found
resting upon his midriff with his fore and hind feet suspended over the opposite sides of some huge log. "The spirit

LITTLE INVULNERABLE.

indeed is willing, but the flesh is weak."   He has an am-
bitious spirit, which is exceeded only by his patience.   He
has had many mishaps, any one of which would have per-
manently disabled a larger animal, and we have dubbed him

"Little Invulnerable." One of the soldiers of our escort, Private Moore, has made a sketch of him as he appeared to-day lying across a log, of which I am to have a copy.

I growled at Hauser and scolded him a little in camp to-night because of some exasperating action of his. I here record the fact without going into details. I think that I must try to be more patient. But I am feeling somewhat the fatigue of our journey. However, there is something to be said on the other hand, and that is that there is no one of the party better able to bear its labors and anxieties than I, and therefore I should be the last man to lose my patience.

I know of nothing that can try one's patience more than a trip of any considerable length by wagon train or pack train through an uninhabited region, and the most amiable of our race cannot pass this ordeal entirely unscathed. Persons who are not blessed with uncommon equanimity never get through such a journey without frequent explosions of temper, and seldom without violence. Even education, gentle training and the sharpest of mental discipline do not always so effectually subdue the passions that they may not be aroused into unwonted fury during a long journey through a country filled with obstructions. Philosophy has never found a fitter subject for its exercise than that afforded by the journey we are now making, which obliges the members of our party to strive to relieve each other's burdens.

Friday, September 9.—Last night there occurred an incident which I would gladly blot from these pages, but a faithful record of all the events of camp life in connection with this expedition demands that I omit nothing of interest, nor set down "aught in malice."

Mr. Hedges and I were on guard during the last relief of the night, which extends from the "Wee sma' hours ayont the twal" to daybreak. The night was wearing on when

Hedges, being tempted of one of the Devils which doubtless roam around this sulphurous region, or that perhaps followed Lieutenant Doane and myself down from that "high mountain apart" where the spirits roam, asked me if I was hungry. I replied that such had been my normal condition ever since our larder had perceptibly declined. Mr. Hedges then suggested that, as there was no food already cooked in the camp, we take each a wing of one of the partridges and broil it over our small fire. It was a "beautiful thought," as Judge Bradford of Colorado used to say from the bench when some knotty legal problem relating to a case he was trying had been solved, and was speedily acted upon by both of us. But I was disappointed in finding so little meat on a partridge wing, and believed that Hedges would have chosen a leg instead of a wing, if he had pondered a moment, so I remedied the omission, and, as a result, each roasted a leg of the bird. Soon increase of appetite grew by what it fed on, and the breast of the bird was soon on the broiler.

In the meantime our consciences were not idle, and we were "pricked in our hearts." The result was that we had a vision of the disappointment of our comrades, as each should receive at our morning breakfast his small allotment of but one partridge distributed among so many, and it did not take us long to send the remaining bird to join its mate. Taking into consideration the welfare of our comrades, it seemed the best thing for us to do, and we debated between ourselves whether the birds would be missed in the morning, Hedges taking the affirmative and I the negative side of the question.

This morning when our breakfast was well nigh finished, Mr. Hauser asked "Newt," the head cook, why he had not prepared the partridges for breakfast. "Newt" answered that when he opened the pan this morning the birds had "done gone," and he thought that "Booby" (the dog) had eaten them. Whereupon Hauser pelted the dog with stones and sticks. Hedges and I, nearly bursting with our suppressed laughter, quietly exchanged glances across the table, and the situation became quite intense for us, as we strove to restrain our risibles while listening to the comments of the party on the utter worthlessness of "that dog Booby." Suddenly the camp was electrified by Gillette asking, "Who was on guard last night?" "That's it," said one. "That's where the birds went," said another. This denouement was too much for Hedges and myself, and amid uproarious laughter we made confession, and "Booby" was relieved from his disgrace and called back into the camp, and patted on the head as a "good dog," and he has now more friends in camp than ever before.

Mr. Hauser, who brought down the birds with two well directed shots with his revolver, made from the back of his horse without halting the animal, had expected to have a dainty breakfast, but he is himself too fond of a practical joke to express any disappointment, and no one in the party is more unconcerned at the outcome than he. He is a philosopher, and, as I know from eight years' association with him, does not worry over the evils which he can remedy, nor those which he cannot remedy. There can be found no better man than he for such a trip as we are making.

"Booby" is taking more kindly, day by day, to the buckskin moccasins which "Newt" made and tied on his feet a few days ago. When he was first shod with them he rebelled and tore them off with his teeth, but I think he has discovered that they lessen his sufferings, which shows that he has some good dog sense left, and that probably his name "Booby" is a misnomer. I think there is a great deal of good in the animal. He is ever on the alert for unusual noises or sounds, and the assurance which I have that he

will give the alarm in case any thieving Indians shall approach our camp in the night is a great relief to my anxiety
lest some straggling band of the Crows may "set us afoot."
Jake Smith was on guard three nights ago, and he was so
indifferent to the question of safety from attack that he en-

JAKE SMITH,
GUARDING THE CAMP
FROM HOSTILE INDIAN ATTACK.
"REQUIESCAT IN PACE."

joyed a comfortable nap while doing guard duty, and I have
asked our artist, Private Moore, to make for me a sketch
of Smith as I found him sound asleep with his saddle for
a pillow. Jake might well adopt as a motto suitable for his
guidance while doing guard duty, "Requiescat in pace."
Doubtless Jake thought, "Shall I not take mine ease in mine

inn?" I say *thought* for I doubt if Jake can give a correct verbal rendering of the sentence. A few evenings ago he jocosely thought to establish, by a quotation from Shakespeare, the unreliability of a member of our party who was telling what seemed a "fish story," and he clinched his argument by adding that he would apply to the case the words of the immortal Shakespeare, "Othello's *reputation's* gone."

We broke camp this morning with the pack train at 10 o'clock, traveling in a westerly course for about two miles, when we gradually veered around to a nearly easterly direction, through fallen timber almost impassable in the estimation of pilgrims, and indeed pretty severe on our pack horses, for there was no trail, and, while our saddle horses with their riders could manage to force their way through between the trees, the packs on the pack animals would frequently strike the trees, holding the animals fast or compelling them to seek some other passage. Frequently, we were obliged to re-arrange the packs and narrow them, so as to admit of their passage between the standing trees. At one point the pack animals became separated, and with the riding animals of a portion of the party were confronted with a prostrate trunk of a huge tree, about four feet in diameter, around which it was impossible to pass because of the obstructions of fallen timber. Yet pass it we must; and the animals, one after another, were brought up to the log, their breasts touching it, when Williamson and I, the two strongest men of the party, on either side of an animal, stooped down, and, placing each a shoulder back of a fore leg of a horse, rose to an erect position, while others of the party placed his fore feet over the log, which he was thus enabled to scale. In this way we lifted fifteen or twenty of our animals over the log.

Soon after leaving our camp this morning our "Little Invulnerable," while climbing a steep rocky ascent, missed his footing and turned three back summersaults down into the bottom of the ravine. We assisted him to his feet without removing his pack, and he seemed none the worse for his adventure, and quickly regained the ridge from which he had fallen and joined the rest of the herd.

At 3 o'clock in the afternoon we halted for the day, having traveled about six miles, but our camp to-night is not more than three miles from our morning camp.

Mr. Hedges' pack horse, "Little Invulnerable," was missing when we camped; and, as I was one of the four men detailed for the day to take charge of the pack train, I returned two miles on our trail with the two packers, Reynolds and Bean, in search of him. We found him wedged between two trees, evidently enjoying a rest, which he sorely needed after his remarkable acrobatic feat of the morning. We are camped in a basin not far from the lake, which surrounds us on three sides—east, north and west. Mr. Everts has not yet come into camp, and we fear that he is lost.

About noon we crossed a small stream that flows towards the southwest arm of the lake, but which, I think, is one of the headwater streams of Snake river. I think that we have crossed the main divide of the Rocky Mountains twice to-day. We have certainly crossed it once, and if we have not crossed it twice we are now camped on the western slope of the main divide. If the creek we crossed about noon to-day continues to flow in the direction it was running at the point where we crossed it, it must discharge into the southwest arm of the lake, and it seems probable that Mr. Everts has followed down this stream.

I have just had a little talk with Lieutenant Doane. He thinks that our camp to-night is on the Snake river side of the main divide, and there are many things that incline me to believe that he is correct in his opinion.*

Last night we had a discussion, growing out of the fact that Hedges and Stickney, for a brief time, were lost, for the purpose of deciding what course we would adopt in case any other member of the party were lost, and we agreed that in such case we would all move on as rapidly as possible to the southwest arm of the lake, where there are hot springs (the vapor of which we noticed from our camp of September 5th), and there remain until all the party were united. Everts thought a better way for a lost man would be to strike out nearly due west, hoping to reach the headwaters of the Madison river, and follow that stream as his guide to the settlements; but he finally abandoned this idea and adopted that which has been approved by the rest of the party. So if Mr. Everts does not come into camp to-night, we will to-morrow start for the appointed rendezvous.

Saturday, September 10.—We broke camp about 10 o'clock this morning, taking a course of about ten degrees north of west, traveling seven miles, and coming to camp on the lake shore at about five miles in a direct line from our morning camp at half past two p. m. No sign of Mr. Everts has been seen to-day, and on our arrival in camp, Gillette and Trumbull took the return track upon the shore of the lake, hoping to find him, or discover some sign of him. A large fire was built on a high ridge commanding all points on the beach, and we fired signal guns from time to time throughout the night.

Mr. Hauser and I ascended a high point overlooking our camp, and about eight hundred feet above it, where from the top of a tall tree I had a fairly good view of the shore

---

*Our subsequent journeying showed that Lieutenant Doane was right in his conjecture.

outline of the west and south shores of the lake, with all the inlets, points and islands. We were also enabled to mark out our course of travel which it would be necessary to follow in order to reach the most southwesterly arm of the lake and take advantage of openings in the timber to facilitate travel. On this high point we built a large fire which could be seen for many miles in all directions by any one not under the bank of the lake, and which we hoped Mr. Everts might see, and so be directed to our camp.

In going to the summit we traveled several hundred feet on a rocky ridge not wide enough for safe travel by a man on horseback. At an elevation of about eight hundred feet above Yellowstone lake we found two small lakes nestled in a deep recess in the mountain and surrounded by the overturned rocks.

Our route to-day has been entirely through fallen timber, and it has been a hard day of travel on our horses, necessitating jumping over logs and dead branches of trees, and thus we have made very slow progress.

The map of Yellowstone lake which we will be enabled to complete from the observations made to-day will show that its shape is very different from that shown on Captain Raynolds' map. The lake has but three islands.

We are more than ever anxious about Mr. Everts. We had hoped, this morning, to make our camp to-night on the southwest arm of the lake, but the fallen timber has delayed us in our travel and prevented our doing so. The southwest arm of the lake has been our objective point for the past three days, and we feel assured that Mr. Everts, finding himself lost, will press on for that point, and, as he will not be hindered by the care of a pack train, he can travel twice as far in one day as we can, and we are therefore the more anxious to reach our destination. We have carefully considered all the points in the case, and have unanimously

decided that it will be utter folly to remain in camp here, and equally so to have remained in this morning's camp, hoping that he would overtake us. On the evening that Mr. Hedges was lost, Mr. Everts told him that he ought to have struck out for the lake, as he (Everts) would do if lost. So we will move on to the southwest arm of the lake and remain three or four days. If Mr. Everts overtakes us at all he will do so by that time.

Sunday, September 11.—Gillette and Trumbull returned to camp this morning, having traversed the shore of the lake to a point east of our camp of September 9th, without discovering any sign of Mr. Everts. We have arrived at the conclusion that he has either struck out for the lake on the west, or followed down the stream which we crossed the day he was lost, or that he is possibly following us. The latter, however, is not very probable.

Mr. Hauser, Lieutenant Doane and I saddled up immediately after breakfast, and, with a supply of provisions for Mr. Everts, pressed forward in advance of the rest of the party, marking a trail for the pack animals through the openings in the dense woods, and avoiding, as far as possible, the fallen timber. We rode through with all possible dispatch, watching carefully for the tracks of a horse, but found no sign of Mr. Everts. We followed both the beach and the trail on the bank for several miles in either direction, but we saw neither sign nor track. The small stream which we crossed on the 9th does not flow into this arm of the lake as we thought it might, and it is evidently a tributary of the Snake river.

The pack train arrived early in the afternoon with the rest of the party, and all were astonished and saddened that no trace of Mr. Everts had been found. We shall to-night mature a plan for a systematic search for him. It is probable that we will make this camp the base of operations, and remain here several days. Everts has with him a supply of matches, ammunition and fishing tackle, and if he will but travel in a direct line and not veer around to the right or left in a circle, he will yet be all right.

Directly west of our camp on the further side of this arm of the lake, and about four miles distant, are several hot springs which we shall visit before leaving the lake.

We were roused this morning about 2 o'clock by the shrill howl of a mountain lion, and again while we were at breakfast we heard another yell. As we stood around our campfire to-night, our ears were saluted with a shriek so terribly human, that for a moment we believed it to be a call from Mr. Everts, and we hallooed in response, and several of our party started in the direction whence the sounds came, and would have instituted a search for our comrade but for an admonitory growl of a mountain lion.

We have traveled to-day about seven miles. On leaving our camps yesterday and to-day, we posted conspicuously at each a placard, stating clearly the direction we had taken and where provisions could be found.

The country through which we have passed for the past five days is like that facetiously described by Bridger as being so desolate and impassable and barren of resources, that even the crows flying over it were obliged to carry along with them supplies of provisions.

Monday, September 12.—In accordance with our pre-arranged programme, three parties were sent out this morning in search of Mr. Everts. Smith and Trumbull were to follow the lake shore until they came in sight of our last camp. Hauser and Gillette were to return on our trail through the woods, taking with them their blankets and two days' rations. General Washburn and myself were to take a southerly direction towards what we called "Brown Mountain," some twelve miles away. Smith and Trumbull returned early in the afternoon and reported having seen in the sand the tracks of a man's foot, and Smith thought that he saw several Indians, who disappeared in the woods as they approached; but Trumbull, who was with him, did not see them, and Smith says it was because he was short-sighted. For some reason they did not pursue their investigations farther, and soon returned in good order to camp.

The reconnaissance made by General Washburn and myself resulted in no discovery of any trace of Everts. We traveled about eleven miles directly south, nearly to the base of Brown mountain, carefully examining the ground the whole of the way, to see if any horseshoe tracks could be discovered. We crossed no stream between the lake and the mountain, and if Mr. Everts followed the stream which we crossed on the 9th, he is south of Brown mountain, for it is evident that he did not pass westward between Brown mountain and Yellowstone lake; otherwise we would have discovered the tracks of his horse.

It is now night, and Hauser and Gillette have not yet returned.

Two miles on this side (the north side) of Brown mountain, Washburn and I passed over a low divide, which, I think, must be the main range of the Rocky Mountains, just beyond which is another brimstone basin containing forty or fifty boiling sulphur and mud springs, and any number of small steam jets. A small creek runs through the basin, and the slopes of the mountains on either side to the height of several hundred feet showed unmistakable signs of volcanic action beneath the crust over which we were traveling. A considerable portion of the slope of the mountain was covered with a hollow incrustation of sulphur and lime, or silica, from which issued in many places hot steam, and we found many small craters from six to twelve inches in diameter, from which issued the sound of the boiling sulphur or mud, and in many instances we could see the mud or sulphur water. There are many other springs of water slightly impregnated with sulphur, in which the water was too hot for us to bear the hand more than two or three seconds, and which overflowed the green spaces between the incrustations, completely saturating the ground, and over which in many places the grass had grown, forming a turf compact and solid enough to bear the weight of a man ordinarily; but when it once gave way the underlying deposit was so thin that it afforded no support. While crossing, heedless of General Washburn's warning, one of these green places, my horse broke through and sank to his body as if in a bed of quicksand. I was off his back in an instant and succeeded in extricating the struggling animal, the turf being strong enough to bear his body alone, without the addition of the weight of a man. The fore legs of my horse, however, had gone through the turf into the hot, thin mud beneath. General Washburn, who was a few yards behind me on an incrusted mound of lime and sulphur (which bore us in all cases), and who had just before called to me to keep off the grassy place, as there was danger beneath it, inquired of me if the deposit beneath the turf was hot. Without making examination I answered that I thought it might be warm. Shortly afterwards the turf again gave way, and my horse plunged more violently than before, throwing me over his head, and, as I fell, my right arm was thrust violently through the treacherous surface into the scalding morass, and it was with difficulty that I rescued my poor horse, and I found it necessary to instantly remove my glove to avoid blistering my hand. The frenzied floundering of my horse had in the first instance suggested to General Washburn the idea that the under stratum was hot enough to scald him. General Washburn was right in his conjecture. It is a fortunate circumstance that I to-day rode my light-weight pack horse; for, if I had ridden my heavy saddle horse, I think that the additional weight of his body would have broken the turf which held up the lighter animal, and that he would have disappeared in the hot boiling mud, taking me with him.

At the base of Brown mountain is a lake, the size of which we could not very accurately ascertain, but which was probably about two miles long by three-quarters of a mile wide. On the south end appeared to be an outlet, and it seems to be near the head of the Snake river. Owing to the difficulty of reaching the beach, growing out of the mishaps arising from the giving way of the turf, as I have described, our nearest approach to the lake was about one-half of a mile.

During the absence of Washburn and myself Mr. Hedges has spent the day in fishing, catching forty of the fine trout with which the lake abounds. Mr. Stickney has to-day made an inventory of our larder, and we find that our luxuries, such as coffee, sugar and flour, are nearly used up, and that we have barely enough of necessary provisions—salt, pepper, etc., to last us ten days longer with economy in their use. We will remain at the lake probably three or four days longer with the hope of finding some trace of Everts, when it will be necessary to turn our faces homewards to avoid general disaster, and in the meantime we will dry a few hundred pounds of trout, and carry them with us as a precautionary measure against starvation. At all of our camps for the past three days, and along the line of travel between them, we have blazed the trees as a guide for Mr. Everts, and have left a small supply of provisions at each place, securely cached, with notices directing Mr. Everts to the places of concealment. The soldiers' rations issued for thirty days' service will barely hold out for their own use, and we have little chance of borrowing from them. We left Helena with thirty days' rations, expecting to be absent but twenty-five days. We have already been journeying twenty-seven days, and are still a long way from home.

A few nights ago I became ravenously hungry while on guard, and ate a small loaf of bread, one of five loaves that I found in a pan by the camp-fire. I was not aware at the time that these loaves were a part of the soldiers' breakfast rations, nor did I know that in the army service each soldier has his own particular ration of bread. So the next morning, with one ration of bread missing, one soldier would have been short in his allowance if the others had not shared their loaves with him. I supposed at the time of my discovery of the five loaves that they belonged to the larder of the Washburn branch of the party—not to the escort—and I apologized to the soldiers when I learned the truth, and we are now as good friends as ever; but, from an occasional remark which they drop in my presence, I perceive that they think they have the laugh on me. Unfortunately for them, we will part company before we reach the settlements, and I will have no opportunity to *liquid*ate my obligations. Hard work and plain living have already reduced my superfluous flesh, and "my clothes like a lady's loose gown hang about me," as the old song runs.

Day before yesterday Mr. Gillette and I discussed the question of the probability of a man being able to sustain life in this region, by depending for his subsistence upon whatever roots or berries are to be found here. We have once before to-day referred to the fact that we have seen none of the roots which are to be found in other parts of the Rocky Mountain region, and especially in the elevated valleys. We have not noticed on this trip a single growing plant or specimen of the camas, the cowse, or yamph. If Mr. Everts has followed the stream on which we were camped the day he was lost down into the Snake river valley, he will find an abundance of the camas root, which is most nutritious, and which will sustain his life if he has sufficient knowledge of the root to distinguish the edible from the poisonous plant.

I have been told by James Stuart that in the valley of the Snake river the "camas" and the "cowse" roots are to be found in great abundance, and are much prized as food by the Indians. "Cowse" is a Nez Perce word, the Snake Indians give the name "thoig" to the same root. It grows in great abundance in the country of the Nez Perce Indians, who eat great quantities of it, and these Indians are called by the Snake Indians the "Thoig A-rik-ka," or "Cowse-eaters." The camas is both flour and potatoes for several wandering nations, and it is found in the most barren and desolate regions in greatest quantity. The camas is a small round root, not unlike an onion in appearance. It is sweet to the taste, full of gluten, and very satisfying to a hungry man. The Indians have a mode of preparing it which makes it very relishable. In a hole a foot in depth, and six feet in diameter, from which the turf has been carefully removed, they build a fire for the purpose of heating the exposed earth surface, while in another fire they heat at the same time a sufficient number of flat rocks to serve as a cover. After the heating process is completed, the roots are spread over the bottom of the hole, covered with the turf with the grass side down, the heated rocks spread above, and a fire built upon them, and the process of cooking produces about the same change in the camas that is produced in coffee by roasting. It also preserves it in a suitable form for ready use.

The yamph has a longer and smaller bulb than the camas, though not quite as nutritious, and may be eaten raw. Either of these roots contains nutriment sufficient to support life, and often in the experience of the tribes of the mountains winters have been passed with no other food. There is a poisonous camas, which is sometimes mistaken for the genuine root, but which cannot be eaten in large quantities without fatal results. It always grows where the true camas is found, and much care is necessary to avoid mixing the two while gathering the roots in any considerable quantity. So great is the esteem in which the camas is held that many of the important localities of the country in which it is found are named for it.*

SECTION OF FUNNEL-SHAPED SPRING.

SHOWING HOW BRANCHES AND TWIGS LODGE AT THE POINT OF CONVERGENCE SO AS TO MAKE A FOUNDATION FOR GRASS AND EARTH UNTIL THE SPRING IS FILLED TO THE TOP AND THE SURFACE IS COVERED WITH A LIVING TURF STRONG ENOUGH TO BEAR A CONSIDERABLE WEIGHT.

Lieutenant Doane was much amazed at the appearance of my horse's legs, upon our return from Brown mountain, and

---

*The Honorable Granville Stuart, of Montana, in his book "Montana as It Is," published in 1865, says that there is another root found in portions of Montana which I have never seen. Mr. Stuart says:

"Thistle-root is the root of the common thistle, which is very abundant in the bottoms along nearly all the streams in the moun-

has asked General Washburn and myself what can be the nature of the ground where such a mishap could occur.   My theory of the matter is this: We frequently found springs of hot water—though not boiling—some fifteen or twenty feet in diameter at the top, the sides of which were funnel-

BREAKING THROUGH THE TURF,

FORMED OVER THE SURFACE OF SUCH A SPRING AS THAT
SHOWN ON THE OPPOSITE PAGE.

shaped, and converged to a narrow opening of say three feet diameter at a depth of twelve or fifteen feet, and which be-

---

tain.   They grow to about the size of a large radish, and taste very much like turnips, and are good either raw or cooked with meat."

Captain William Clark, of the famous Lewis and Clark expedition, dropped the final *e* from the word cowse, spelling it c-o-w-s. Unless this error is noticed by the reader, he will not understand what Captain Clark meant when he said that members of his party were searching for the *cows*.

low the point of convergence opened out like an hour glass. In some of these springs at the point of convergence we found tree branches that had fallen into the spring and had become impregnated with the silica or lime of the water; water-soaked we call it. I saw a number of such springs in which several branches of trees were lying across the small opening at the point of convergence. When once these are firmly lodged, they form a support for smaller branches and twigs, and thus the tufts of grass which the spring floods or melting snows bring down from the sides of the mountain will, after a few years, made a sufficiently strong foundation for the earth, which will also wash down the slopes into the spring. Once a firm footing is established, it is only a question of time when the spring will be filled to the brim with earth. Then gradually the seed blown over the surface of the spring from the weeds and grass near by will take root, and, in the course of a few years, a strong turf will be formed, through which the water may percolate in many places, though giving to the unsuspecting traveler no sign of its treacherous character. I think that it was through such a turf as this that the fore legs of my horse and my right hand were plunged.*

My pack horse which I rode to-day, a buckskin colored broncho, which is docile under the pack saddle, "bucked" as I mounted him this morning; but I kept my seat in the saddle without difficulty. Walter Trumbull, however, on my return to-night, presented me with a sketch which he says is a faithful portrayal of both horse and rider in the

---

*Lieutenant Doane, in his official report to the War Department, says, concerning this episode:

"Washburn and Langford * * * became entangled in an immense swampy brimstone basin, abounding in sulphur springs. * * * Mr. Langford's horse broke through several times, coming back plastered with the white substance and badly scalded."

acrobatic act. I think the sketch is an exaggeration, and that I hugged the saddle in better form than it indicates.

Tuesday, September 13.—It was Jake Smith's turn to stand guard last night, but he refused to do so, and Washburn took his place.

MY BUCKING BRONCHO.

We have remained in camp all day. At about 9 o'clock this morning it began to rain and hail, and we have had a little snow, which continued to fall at intervals all day. At about 6 o'clock this evening Hauser and Gillette arrived in camp, having returned on the trail to within three miles of the place where we camped on the night of September 7th. They examined the trail and the beach with the utmost care, but without discovering any trace of Mr. Everts. They say that the trail over which our train passed, or, rather, the path which our train made, was hardly plain enough to be followed, and in many places where the pine leaves had fallen thick upon the ground, it was totally invisible, so that no one could have followed it with certainty except by dismounting and closely observing the ground at every step. They made the journey very well, from the fact that they had traveled the route once before, and their horses instinctively followed the back path for a great part of the distance without any special guidance. On their near approach to camp, when the trail was no longer discernible, their dog "Booby" took the lead when they were at fault, and brought them into camp all right. They think they might have been forced to lie out all night but for the sagacity of "Booby." They made on each of the two days nearly as great a distance as our train traveled in four days. Their report has fully set at rest the question of Mr. Everts having followed us. It settles as a fact that he did not again strike our trail, and that had he done so he could not have followed it, owing to his short-sightedness. Hauser and Gillette are probably the two best trailers and woodsmen in our party, and their report of the condition of the trail and the difficulty experienced in following it has satisfied us that Mr. Everts has either struck off in a southerly direction, following perhaps the headwaters of the Snake river, or that he has made an effort to reach the head of the lake with a view of returning by our trail to Boteler's ranch. It is snowing hard to-night, and the prospect for a day or two more in this camp is very good. The murky atmosphere to-night brings to view a number of springs on the opposite shore of this arm of the lake and farther back in the hills which we have not heretofore seen, and the steam is rising from fifty craters in the timbered ridge, giving it the appearance of a New England factory village.

After holding a council this evening we have resolved to remain at this place two days more, hoping that Mr. Everts may overtake us, this arm of the lake being the *objective point* of our travel, fixed on the day before that on which Mr. Everts was lost.

Wednesday, September 14.—We have remained in camp all day, as it is next to impossible to move. The snow is nearly two feet deep, and is very wet and heavy, and our horses are pawing in it for forage. Our large army tent is doing us good service, and, as there is an abundance of dry wood close by our camp, we are extremely comfortable. I am the only one of the party who has a pair of water-proof boots, and I was up and out of the tent this morning before daylight cutting into cordwood a pine log, and before noon I had more than a half cord at the tent door. Washburn and Hauser offered to do some of this work if I would loan them my water-proof boots; but, as they are of a full size for me, and would probably drop off of their feet, I told them that I would get the wood.

Lieutenant Doane to-day requested me to loan him this diary from which to write up his records, as the condition of his thumb has interfered with his use of a pen or pencil. I have accordingly loaned it to him, and Private Moore has been busy the greater part of the day copying portions of it.

For myself, I am very glad to have a day of rest, for I have felt much wearied for several days. I think that I am certainly within bounds when I say that I have put in sixteen hours a day of pretty hard work, attending to camp duties, and writing each day till late at night, and I realize that this journal of travel is becoming ponderous. Yet there is daily crowded upon my vision so much of novelty and wonder, which should be brought to the notice of the world, and which, so far as my individual effort is concerned, will be lost to it if I do not record the incidents of each day's travel, that I am determined to make my journal as full as possible, and to purposely omit no details. It is a lifetime opportunity for publishing to all who may be interested a complete record of the discoveries of an expedition which in coming time will rank among the first and most important of American explorations.

It is cold to-night, and the water in a pail standing at our tent door was frozen at 7 o'clock in the evening.

The water fowl are more abundant at this point than they have been elsewhere on the lake on our journey around it, and we could see to-day hundreds of swans, geese and ducks, and many pelicans and gulls.

Thursday, September 15.—This forenoon the weather moderated, and one-half the snow has melted, so that it is but about ten inches deep to-night. Still, our horses are becoming restless for want of sufficient food. The patches of grass which may be found under the snow are very limited in extent, and as the animals are confined to the length of their lariats, foraging is much more difficult than if they were running loose. We have seen no signs of Indians following us since we made our first camp upon the lake, and but little evidence that they have ever been here, except some few logs piled so as to conceal from view a hunter who may be attempting to bring down some of the game swimming on the lake. We feel convinced that Jake Smith drew upon both his imagination and his fears three days ago, when he reported that he had seen Indians on the beach of the lake.

Each night that we have been camped here we have heard the shrill cries of the mountain lions, and under a momentary illusion I have each time been half convinced that it was a human being in distress. Because of the mountain lions we are keeping close watch upon our horses. They are very fond of horse flesh, and oftentimes will follow a horse-

LIEUT. GUSTAVUS C. DOANE.

JACK BARONETTE.

man a long distance, more to make a meal upon the flesh of the horse than for the purpose of attacking the rider.

During the three days we have spent in this camp, I have been enabled to complete my diary for September 8th, 9th and 10th, which were red letter days—days of great anxiety.

I had a good nap this afternoon while my diary was being used for Lieutenant Doane, and I feel greatly refreshed. My first thought on awakening was for poor Everts. I wonder where he can be throughout all this fierce storm and deep snow! Perhaps the snow did not reach him, for I noticed to-night that the ground was quite bare on the opposite side of this arm of the lake, while the snow is eight or ten inches deep here at our camp. Hauser is not feeling very well to-night.

Friday, September 16.—We this morning resolved to move over to the vicinity of the hot springs on the opposite side of this arm of the lake, from which point we will leave the Yellowstone for the Madison river or some one of its branches. We followed up the beach for half a mile, and then journeyed along the bank of the lake through the woods for a mile to avoid the quicksands on the lake shore; then, taking the beach again, we followed it to the springs where we are now camped.*

These springs surpass in extent, variety and beauty any which we have heretofore seen. They extend for the distance of nearly a mile along the shore of the lake, and back from the beach about one hundred yards. They number between ninety and one hundred springs, of all imaginable varieties. Farthest from the beach are the springs of boiling mud, in some of which the mud is very thin, in others of such a consistency that it is heaped up as it boils over, gradu-

---

*The location of this camp is what is now called the "Thumb" station on the stage route.

ally spreading under its own weight until it covers quite a large surface. The mud or clay is of different colors. That in some of the springs is nearly as white as white marble; in others it is of a lavender color; in others it is of a rich pink, of different shades. I have taken specimens of each, which I will have analyzed on my return home.* In close proximity to these are springs discharging water nearly clear and apparently odorless, the bottoms and sides of which, as well as of the channels of the streams running from them, are covered with soft deposits of some substance they contain in solution. These deposits and the hard incrustations around the edges of the springs are of various colors, in some cases being dark red, in others scarlet, in others yellow, and in still others green.

Along the shore of the lake are several boiling springs situated in the top of incrusted craters, but which do not boil over, the sediment which has been deposited around them forming a wall or embankment, holding back the water.

But the most remarkable of all the springs at this point are six or seven of a character differing from any of the rest. The water in them is of a dark blue or ultra-marine hue, but it is wonderfully clear and transparent. Two of these springs are quite large; the remaining five are smaller, their diameters ranging from eight to fifteen feet. The water in

---

*Analyses of the various specimens of mud taken from the springs in this locality, made on our return to Helena, gave the following results:

White Sediment.		Lavender Sediment.		Pink Sediment.	
Silica	42.2	Silica	28.2	Silica	32.6
Magnesia	33.4	Alumina	58.6	Alumina	52.4
Lime	17.8	Boracic acid	3.2	Oxide of calcium	8.3
Alkalis	6.6	Oxide of iron	0.6	Soda and potassa	4.2
		Oxide of calcium	4.2	Water and loss	2.5
	100.0	Water and loss	5.2		
					100.0
			100.0		

These analyses were made by Professor Augustus Steitz, assayer of the First National Bank of Helena, Mont.

one of these latter is thrown up to the height of two feet. The largest two of these springs are irregular in their general outline of nearly an oval shape, the larger of the two being about twenty-five feet wide by forty long, and the smaller about twenty by thirty feet. The discharge from each of them is about one gallon per minute. The sides of the springs are funnel-shaped, and converge until at the depth of thirty feet, the opening is about eight feet in diameter. From the surface or rim down to the lowest point of convergence where the opening enlarges, the sides of the funnel (which are corrugated and very uneven and irregular) are covered with a white deposit or incrustation which contrasts vividly with the dark opening at its base, which is distinctly visible at the depth of forty feet.   These two springs are distant from each other about twenty yards, and there is a difference of about four feet in the elevation or level of the water.   One peculiar feature of all these springs is that they seem to have no connection with each other beneath the surface.   We find springs situated five or six feet apart, of the same general appearance but of different temperatures, and with the water upon different levels.   The overflow from these springs for a great number of years has formed an incrusted bank overlooking the border of the lake, rising to the height of six feet; and, as the streams running from the springs are bordered with incrustations of various hues, depending upon the nature of the deposit or substance in solution, so the incrusted bank, which has been in process of formation for ages, exhibits all of these varied colors.   In a number of places along the bank of the lake, this incrusted deposit is broken down and has crumbled into small pieces, upon which the waves have dashed until they have been moulded into many curious shapes, and having all the colors of the deposits in the springs—white, red and white blended, yellow and green.   Cavernous hollows which fill the shore incrustation respond in weird and melancholy echoes to the dash of the billows.

The bottoms of the streams flowing from the deeper springs have for some distance a pure white incrustation; farther down the slope the deposit is white in the center with sides of red, and still farther down the white deposit is hidden entirely by the red combined with yellow. From nearly all these springs we obtained specimens of the adjoining incrustations, all of which were too hot to be held for more than a moment even with the gloved hand.

Between the springs all along the border of the lake were small craters from which issued hot steam or vapor, besides which there were many cold craters. Along the edge of the lake, out in the water from ten to thirty feet from the shore are to be found springs with the water bubbling up a few inches above the surface. None of the springs in this locality appeared to be very strongly impregnated with sulphur. Some of the incrustations on the beach are as white and delicate as alabaster. These are the springs which we observed on September 5th from our camp on the eastern shore of the lake.

Our explorations of the Yellowstone will cease at this point, and to-morrow we start in our search for Firehole Basin. Our journey around Yellowstone lake in close proximity to the beach is doubtless the first ever attempted; and, although it has been attended with difficulty and distress, these have been to me as nothing compared with the enjoyment the journey has afforded, and it is with the greatest regret that I turn my face from it homewards. How can I sum up its wonderful attractions! It is dotted with islands of great beauty, as yet unvisited by man, but which at no remote period will be adorned with villas and the ornaments of civilized life. The winds from the mountain gorges roll its placid waters into a furious sea, and crest its billows with foam. Forests of pine, deep, dark and almost impenetrable, are scattered at random along its banks, and its beautiful margin presents every variety of sand and pebbly beach, glittering with crystals, carnelians and chalcedony. The Indians approach it under the fear of a superstition originating in the volcanic forces surrounding it, which amounts almost to entire exclusion. It possesses adaptabilities for the highest display of artificial culture, amid the greatest wonders of Nature that the world affords, and is beautified by the grandeur of the most extensive mountain scenery, and not many years can elapse before the march of civil improvement will reclaim this delightful solitude, and garnish it with all the attractions of cultivated taste and refinement.

Strange and interesting as are the various objects which we have met with in this vast field of natural wonders, no camp or place of rest on our journey has afforded our party greater satisfaction than the one we are now occupying, which is our first camp since emerging from the dense forest. Filled with gloom at the loss of our comrade, tired, tattered, browned by exposure and reduced in flesh by our labors, we resemble more a party of organized mendicants than of men in pursuit of Nature's greatest novelties. But from this point we hope that our journey will be comparatively free from difficulties of travel.

Mr. Hauser's experience as a civil engineer has been an invaluable aid in judging of the "lay of the land," and so in giving direction to our party in its zig-zag journeying around the lake. In speaking of this, Hauser says that he thinks that I have a more correct idea of mountain heights, distances and directions, and can follow a direct course through dense timber more unerringly than any man he knows, except James Stuart—a compliment which I accept most graciously. Some of our party declare that they would have had no expectation of finding their way back

to camp, if they had ventured into the forest in search of
Mr. Everts.

I recited to Washburn and Hauser to-night an extract
from "The Task," by the poet Cowper, which, in my younger
days, I memorized for declamation, and which, I think, is at
once expressive of our experience in the journey around the
lake and of our present relief.

> "As one who long in thickets and in brakes
> Entangled, winds now this way and now that,
> His devious course uncertain, seeking home,
> Or having long in miry ways been foiled
> And sore discomfited, from slough to slough
> Plunging, and half despairing of escape,
> If chance at length he finds a green-sward
> Smooth and faithful to the foot, his spirits rise.
> He chirrups brisk his ear-erecting steed,
> And winds his way with pleasure and with ease."

It is a source of great regret to us all that we must leave
this place and abandon the search for Mr. Everts; but our
provisions are rapidly diminishing, and force of circumstances obliges us to move forward. We still indulge the
hope that he may have found and followed down some
branch of the Madison river and reached Virginia City, or
down Snake river and reached some settlement in that valley; and but for our anxiety to reach home and prove or
disprove our expectations, we might have devoted much
more time to visiting the objects of interest we have seen,
and which we have been obliged to pass by.

Mr. Hauser has eaten nothing to-day, and this evening he
told me that he felt sick. Such an acknowledgment from
him means far more than it would coming from many another man, for I know from intimate association with him

for eight years that there is no man in our party who will more uncomplainingly reconcile himself to the hardships and privations of such a journey as this, and if he is too ill to travel to-morrow morning, and if the rest of our party think that they ought to take up the journey homeward, I will remain with him here for a day, and as the others will have to search out a path through the fallen timber, we can make their two days' journey in one by following their beaten trail without obstacles, and overtake them by the time they reach the Firehole river, if they find it at all.

Saturday, September 17, morning.—We were awakened before daylight this morning by loud roaring sounds proceeding from the hot springs close by our camp, some of which were in violent action, though entirely quiescent yesterday. Some of them in which the surface of the water, last night, was several feet below the rim, are now overflowing.

My saddle horse broke his lariat, frightened by the roaring of the springs, and plunged along too near one of them, when the surrounding incrustation gave way and he sank down to his body, but frantically extricated himself without standing upon the order of his extrication;—but he has cut his foot so badly that I do not think it will be prudent to ride him to-day. In his stead I will ride my smaller pack horse, who has nearly recovered from the effects of the scalding he received on my trip to Brown mountain. The hair has come off his legs in several places as the result of that mishap, yet his wonderful vitality always leaves him in a cheerful frame of mind and ready for any duty.

This has been a gloomy morning in our camp, for we all have been depressed at the thought of leaving the lake and abandoning the search for Mr. Everts. We have discussed the situation from every point of view, and have tried to put ourselves in his place and have considered all the possi-

bilities of fate that may befall him.   At one moment he may
be buoyed up with hope, however faint—at another weighed
down by despair and fear, with all their mental terrors.
Has he met death by accident, or may he be injured and unable to move, and be suffering the horrors of starvation and
fever?   Has he wandered aimlessly hither and thither until
bereft of reason?   As I contemplate all these possibilities,
it is a relief to think that he may have lost his life at the
hand of some vagabond Indian.

As the result of this conference we have decided upon a
final plan of action.   We will give to Gillette from our rem-
nant of provisions, ten days' rations, and Lieutenant Doane
will detail Privates Moore and Williamson, with ten days'
rations, and the three will continue the search from this
point.   Mr. Gillette says that with the ten days' rations
they can devote five days to a continuous search, and the
remaining five days will be sufficient, with forced traveling,
for them to overtake us.

Hauser has endeavored to throw a little cheer into the conference by saying to Gillette:

"I think that I should be willing to take the risk of spending ten days more in this wilderness, if I thought that by so
doing I could find a father-in-law."   This provoked an uproarious shout of laughter, for we well understood that
Hauser alluded to the many social courtesies which Gillette,
in Helena, had extended to Miss Bessie Everts, the charming
daughter of our lost comrade, and one of the most attractive
of Montana belles.   This sally of Mr. Hauser gives to me
the assurance of his own convalescence; and, if it so happens
that Gillette finds Mr. Everts, we will have the realization
of another image in "Childe Harold," "A rapture on the
lonely shore."*

---

*On our return home, finding that no tidings of Mr. Everts had
been received, Jack Baronette and George A. Prichett, two experi-

Saturday, September 17, evening.—Gillette, Moore and Williamson left us this morning about 9 o'clock on their final quest for Mr. Everts, and the rest of our party soon resumed our journey. We have traveled about twelve miles to-day, about one-half of the distance being through open timber, and the other half over prostrate pines unmarked by any trail, and through which we found it difficult to make our way, although the obstructions were not so formidable as those on the south shore of Yellowstone lake.* About noon we crossed a high ridge which we had reached by a steep ascent, and on descending the opposite side we saw upon our left a large lake which Lieutenant Doane and some others of our party think is at the head of Firehole river, and they suggested that we make our way to this lake and take as a guide to the Firehole the stream which they believe

enced trappers and old mountaineers, were provided with thirty days' provisions and dispatched in search of him, and by them Mr. Everts was found on October 16th, after wandering in the forest for thirty-seven days from the time he was lost. From the letter of Mr. Prichett addressed to Mr. Gillette, myself and others, I quote: "We found him on the 16th inst. on the summit of the first big mountain beyond Warm Spring creek, about seventy-five miles from Fort Ellis. He says he subsisted all this time on one snow bird, two small minnows and the wing of a bird which he found and mashed between two stones, and made some broth of in a yeast powder can. This was all, with the exception of thistle roots, he had subsisted on."

The narrative of Mr. Everts, of his thirty-seven days' sojourn in the wilderness (published in Scribner's Magazine for November, 1871, and in volume V. of the Montana Historical Society publications), furnishes a chapter in the history of human endurance, exposure, and escape, almost as incredible as it is painfully instructive and entertaining.

*Our general line of travel from the southwest estuary of the lake (Thumb) to the Firehole river was about one mile south of the present stage route. The tourist who to-day makes the rapid and comfortable tour of the park by stage, looking south from Shoshone Point, may catch a glimpse of a portion of the prostrate forest through and over which we struggled, and thus form some idea of the difficulties which beset us on our journey from the lake to the Firehole river.

will be found flowing from it. They argued that by so doing we would be relieved from all uncertainty concerning the course to be pursued in order to reach the Firehole river; but they were easily persuaded that if the Firehole does take its rise in that lake, we can as certainly strike that river by pursuing our present westwardly direction as if we followed the plan suggested by them. Hauser and I feel sure that this large lake is the head of Snake river.

In the afternoon we passed another ridge and descended into a small open valley where we found a spring of good water, and where we are now camped, near a very small creek, which runs in a direction a little north of west, and which I believe flows to the Firehole or the Madison river. Our direction of travel to-day has been governed somewhat by our compasses, but we have neglected to make allowance for the variation of the magnetic needle, which I think is about twenty degrees east of the true meridian. Therefore in trying to follow a westerly course, we have in reality taken a course about twenty degrees north of west.

As we passed the large lake on our left to-day, I observed that there was no ridge of land between us and the lake; therefore I believe that it is in the Snake river valley, and that we have to-day twice crossed the main range of the Rocky Mountains. The fact that the Snake river valley is so readily accessible from Yellowstone lake, gives me hope to-night that Mr. Everts may have made his way out of the forest to some settlement in the Snake river valley.

There is still four or five inches of snow on the ground, but there is plenty of long grass under it, and our horses are faring tolerably well, and will soon fill themselves with either grass or snow. There is no clear space large enough for us to pitch our tent. We have had our supper—an indifferent and scanty meal—and each man is now seeking with varied success a dry spot beneath the sheltering branches of the pines whereon to spread his blankets.

Some of our party seem terribly fatigued, and others mentally depressed. The question of our present locality is still unsolved in their minds, and has been intensified by the discussions in camp to-night as to whether or not the large lake we saw discharges its waters into the Snake river, and they ask: "If it does so, have we re-crossed the main range to the eastern slope?" For myself I do not know of any day since we left home when I have been in better spirits. I am sure we are on the right course and feel no anxiety.

The sky to-night is clear and cloudless, but the snow is melting fast, and there is a peculiar odor in the air that gives assurance of rain before morning. Hedges (my bed fellow) and I have selected our sleeping place, and I have placed over it a ridge-pole, supported by branches of a tree, and have erected a "wickiup" of green pine boughs overlapping like a thatched roof, which will turn off the rain if it comes, and I have advised the others of our party to make similar preparations for a rain. Hedges says that he feels worried and very much discouraged.

Sunday, September 18, 8 o'clock a. m.—There occurred a half hour ago the first serious mishap affecting the welfare of the entire party; and while the packers, Bean and Reynolds, are repairing the damage resulting therefrom, I will go back a few hours and chronicle in the order of their occurrence the events of the early morning.

Mr. Hedges and I, sleeping securely under the sheltering roof of our pine-thatched wickiup, were aroused from our sweet dreams of home about 4 o'clock this morning by several members of our party, who sought shelter from the rain which came down abundantly, or, as a Westmoreland deacon used to say, "in cupious perfusion." The rain storm broke about 3 o'clock in the morning, and all of the party except

Hedges and myself were well drenched, as their only protection from the rain was their blankets. An effort had been made by some of the party to kindle a fire under the shelter of a large standing tree, but with indifferent success. Hedges and I crawled out of our dry blankets, and sat upright, so as to make as much room as possible for the others, and we welcomed all our comrades to our dry shelter. General Washburn, who is suffering somewhat from a cold, was especially grateful for the protection from the storm, which continued until about 7 o'clock. The roof of our wickiup had completely protected Hedges and myself from the rain except at one spot directly over Hedges' exposed ear, where a displacement of the pine leaves allowed a small stream to trickle through the roof, filling his ear with water, much to his discomfort.

Some members of our party, at our early breakfast this morning, sitting upon logs at various distances from our camp fire in their half-dried clothing, and eating their scanty meal in silence, presented a sorry appearance. Some are disappointed that we did not, last night, reach the Firehole river, or some large branch of the Madison, which may guide us homeward, and are wondering if we are moving in the right direction. I feel so perfectly confident that we are traveling the right course that I am in the best of spirits. It may be that my cheerfulness is owing, in some degree, to my having dry clothing and a dry skin, which few of my comrades have, but I see no reason for discouragement. I think that Mr. Hauser is the best and most accurate judge of distances, of heights of mountains, and direction of travel, of any man I know, and he does not doubt that we are moving in the right direction. It is a satisfaction to have my opinion confirmed by his judgment.

We had just finished our breakfast a half hour ago when something—some wild animal, or, perhaps, a snake—moving

Nathaniel P. Langford

in the brush near where our horses were picketed, frightened three of them, and in their violent plunging they pulled up the iron picket pins attached to their lariats, and dashed at a gallop directly through our camp, over the campfire, and upsetting and scattering hither and thither our cooking utensils. The iron picket pins flying through the air at the lariat ends narrowly missed several of our party, but became entangled with the only two sound pack saddles remaining of the entire number with which we started, and dashed them against the adjacent trees, tearing off the side pieces of the saddletrees, and rendering them useless. Our first thought was that the damage done was beyond repair. We had, however, a few thin boards, the remnants of our canned goods boxes, and from my seamless sack of personal baggage I produced two gimlets, a screwdriver, a pair of nippers, some wrought nails and two dozens of screws of various sizes. When all these things were laid out, my comrades expressed great surprise, for not one of them or the packers had any idea that there were any tools or screws in our "outfit." On the other hand, it is a matter of surprise to me that I am the only member of our party who has a rubber coat, or a pair of oil-tanned water-proof boots, or who has brought with him any medicines, tools, screws, etc.; and, except myself, there is but one member of our party (whom I will not "give away" by here recording his name) who had the foresight to bring with him a flask of whiskey. I think we will be known among those who will hereafter visit this marvelous region as "The Temperance Party," though some of our number who lacked the foresight to provide, before leaving Helena, a needed remedy for snake bites, have not lacked the hindsight required in using it.

Bean and Reynolds have just announced that the pack saddles have been repaired, and that preparations are being made for the start, so on this hint I suspend my record until night.

Sunday, September 18, evening.—We left our morning camp about 9 o'clock, pursuing our uncertain course through fallen timber for a distance of about three miles, when we had all our fears of misdirection relieved by coming suddenly upon the banks of the Firehole river, the largest fork of the Madison, down which we followed five miles, passing several groups of boiling springs and a beautiful cascade* (to which we gave no name), when we emerged from the dense forest into a sequestered basin two miles above the union of the Firehole river with a stream which comes in from the southwest, the basin extending to the width of a mile, and traversing the river until contracted between proximate ranges two miles below our camp.

I have spent the entire afternoon and part of this evening in examining the geysers and springs, but will not further record the explorations of to-day until we are ready to leave the basin.

Monday, September 19.—When we left Yellowstone lake two days ago, the desire for home had superceded all thought of further explorations. Five days of rapid travel would, we believed, bring us to the upper valley of the Madison, and within twenty-five miles of Virginia City, and we indulged the remote hope that we might there find some trace of Mr. Everts. We had within a distance of fifty miles seen what we believed to be the greatest wonders on the continent. We were convinced that there was not on the globe another region where within the same limits Nature had crowded so much of grandeur and majesty with so much of novelty and wonder. Judge, then, of our astonishment on entering this basin, to see at no great distance before us an immense

---

*Called now Kepler's cascade.

body of sparkling water, projected suddenly and with terrific force into the air to the height of over one hundred feet. We had found a real geyser. In the valley before us were a thousand hot springs of various sizes and character, and five hundred craters jetting forth vapor. In one place the eye followed through crevices in the crust a stream of hot water of considerable size, running at nearly right angles with the river, and in a direction, not towards, but away from the stream. We traced the course of this stream by the crevices in the surface for twenty or thirty yards. It is probable that it eventually flows into the Firehole, but there is nothing on the surface to indicate to the beholder the course of its underground passage to the river.

On the summit of a cone twenty-five feet high was a boiling spring seven feet in diameter, surrounded with beautiful incrustations, on the slope of which we gathered twigs encased in a crust a quarter of an inch in thickness. On an incrusted hill opposite our camp are four craters from three to five feet in diameter, sending forth steam jets and water to the height of four or five feet. But the marvelous features of this wonderful basin are its spouting geysers, of which during our brief stay of twenty-two hours we have seen twelve in action. Six of these threw water to the height of from fifteen to twenty feet, but in the presence of others of immense dimensions they soon ceased to attract attention.

Of the latter six, the one we saw in action on entering the basin ejected from a crevice of irregular form, and about four feet long by three wide, a column of water of corresponding magnitude to the height of one hundred feet. Around this crevice or mouth the sediment is piled in many capricious shapes, chiefly indented globules from six inches to two feet in diameter. Little hollows in the crust filled with water contained small white spheres of tufa, of the size of a nutmeg, formed as it seemed to me around some nuclei.*

We gave such names to those of the geysers which we saw in action as we think will best illustrate their peculiarities. The one I have just described General Washburn has named "Old Faithful," because of the regularity of its eruptions, the intervals between which being from sixty to sixty-five minutes, the column of water being thrown at each eruption to the height of from eighty to one hundred feet.

---

*An incident of so amusing a character occurred soon after my return to Helena, that I cannot forbear narrating it here. Among the specimens of silica which I brought home were several dark globules about the size of nutmegs. I exhibited these to a noted physician of Helena, Dr. Hovaker, and soon after the return of Mr. Gillette from his search for Mr. Everts, I called upon him at his store and exhibited to him these specimens of silica. At the same time I took a nutmeg from a box upon the store counter, and playfully asked Gillette, in the presence of Dr. Hovaker, if he had found any of those singular incrustations. Dr. Hovaker, believing of course that the specimen I held in my hand came from the Yellowstone, took the nutmeg, and with wonder exhibited in every feature, proceeded to give it a critical examination, frequently exclaiming: "How very like it is to a nutmeg." He finally took a nutmeg from a box near by, and balanced the supposed incrustation with it, declaring the former to be the lighter. Asking my permission to do so, he took the nutmeg (which he supposed to be an incrustation) to a jeweler in the vicinity, and broke it. The aroma left him no doubt as to its character, but he was still deceived as to its origin. When I saw him returning to the store, in anticipation of the reproof I should receive, I started for the rear door; but the Doctor, entering before I reached it, called me back, and in a most excited manner declared that we had discovered real nutmegs, and nutmegs of a very superior quality. He had no doubt that Yellowstone lake was surrounded by nutmeg trees, and that each of our incrustations contained a veritable nutmeg. In his excitement he even proposed to organize a small party to go immediately to the locality to gather nutmegs, and had an interview with Charley Curtis on the subject of furnishing pack animals for purposes of transportation. When, on the following day, he ascertained the truth, after giving me a characteristic lecture, he revenged himself by good naturedly conferring upon the members of our party the title, by which he always called them thereafter, of "Nutmegs."

N. P. LANGFORD.

The "Fan" has a distorted pipe from which are projected two radiating sheets of water to the height of sixty feet, resembling a feather fan. Forty feet from this geyser is a vent connected with it, two feet in diameter, which, during

OLD FAITHFUL.
NAMED BY GENERAL WASHBURN.

the eruption, expels with loud reports dense volumes of vapor to the height of fifty feet.

The "Grotto," so named from the singularly winding apertures penetrating the sinter surrounding it, was at rest when we first discovered it. Externally it presented few indications of its character as a geyser. Private Williamson, one of our escort, crawled through an aperture and looked into the discharging orifice. When afterwards, he saw it belching forth a column of boiling water two feet in diameter to the height of sixty feet, and a scalding stream of two hundred square inches flowing from the cavern he had entered a short time before, he said that he felt like one who had narrowly escaped being summarily cooked.

The "Castle" is on the summit of an incrusted elevation. This name was given because of its resemblance to the ruins of some old tower with its broken down turrets. The silicious sinter composing the formation surrounding it takes the form of small globules, resembling a ripe cauliflower, and the massive nodules indicate that at some former period the flow of water must have been much larger than at present. The jet is sixty feet high by four feet in diameter, and the vent near it, which is in angry ebullition during the eruption, constantly flows with boiling water.

One of the most wonderful of the springs in this basin is that of ultra-marine hue directly in front of the "Castle" geyser. It is nearly round, having diameters of about twenty and twenty-five feet, the sides being corrugated and funnel-shaped, and at the depth of thirty feet opening out into a cavern of unfathomable depth, the rim of the spring having beautifully escalloped edges. It does not boil over, but a very small stream of water flows from it, and it is not affected in its appearance by the spouting of the geyser in its immediate proximity. There is evidently no connection between this spring and the geyser.

The "Giant" is a rugged deposit presenting in form a miniature model of the Colosseum. It has an opening three feet in diameter. A remarkable characteristic of this geyser is the duration of its discharges, which yesterday afternoon continued for more than an hour in a steady stream about three feet in diameter and one hundred and forty feet high.

Opposite our camp, on the east side of the Firehole river, is a symmetrical cone resembling an old-fashioned straw beehive with the top cut off. It is about five feet in diameter at its base, with an irregular oval-shaped orifice having escalloped edges, and of twenty-four by thirty-six inches interior diameter. No one supposed that it was a geyser, and until this morning, among so many wonders, it had escaped a second notice. Suddenly, while we were at breakfast this morning, a column of water shot from it, which by quite accurate triangular measurement proved to be two hundred and nineteen feet in height. Our method of triangulation was as follows: A point on the surface of the ground was marked, which was in a direct line with a branch of a tree near by, and of the top of the column of water when at its greatest height. Having obtained the perpendicular height of the branch of the tree from the ground, and the distance from this perpendicular to the point of observation and to the geyser cone, we were enabled to make a very accurate calculation of the height of the column of water. We named this geyser the "Bee Hive."

Near by is situated the "Giantess," the largest of all the geysers we saw in eruption. Ascending a gentle slope for a distance of sixty yards we came to a sink or well of an irregular oval shape, fifteen by twenty feet across, into which we could see to the depth of fifty feet or more, but could discover no water, though we could distinctly hear it gurgling and boiling at a fearful rate afar down this vertical cavern. Suddenly it commenced spluttering and rising with incredible rapidity, causing a general stampede among our company, who all moved around to the windward side of the geyser. When the water had risen within about twenty-five feet of the surface, it became stationary, and we returned to look down upon the foaming water, which occasionally emitted hot jets nearly to the mouth of the orifice. As if tired of this sport the water began to ascend at the rate of five feet in a second, and when near the top it was expelled with terrific momentum in a column the full size of the immense aperture to a height of sixty feet. The column remained at this height for the space of about a minute, when from the apex of this vast aqueous mass five lesser jets or round columns of water varying in size from six to fifteen inches in diameter shot up into the atmosphere to the amazing height of two hundred and fifty feet. This was without exception the most magnificent phenomenon I ever beheld. We were standing on the side of the geyser exposed to the sun, whose sparkling rays filled the ponderous column with what appeared to be the clippings of a thousand rainbows. These prismatic illusions disappeared, only to be succeeded by myriads of others which continually fluttered and sparkled through the spray during the twenty minutes the eruption lasted. These lesser jets, thrown so much higher than the main column and shooting through it, doubtless proceed from auxiliary pipes leading into the principal orifice near the bottom, where the explosive force is greater. The minute globules into which the spent column was diffused when falling sparkled like a shower of diamonds, and around every shadow produced by the column of steam hiding the sun was the halo so often represented in paintings as encircling the head of the Savior. We unhesitatingly agreed that this was the greatest wonder of our trip.

Mr. Hedges and I forded the Firehole river a short distance below our camp. The current, as it dashed over the boulders, was swift, and, taking off our boots and stockings, we selected for our place of crossing what seemed to be a smooth rock surface in the bottom of the stream, extending from shore to shore. When I reached the middle of the stream I paused a moment and turned around to speak to Mr. Hedges, who was about entering the stream, when I discovered from the sensation of warmth under my feet that I was standing upon an incrustation formed over a hot spring that had its vent in the bed of the stream. I exclaimed to Hedges: "Here is the river which Bridger said was *hot at the bottom*."*

How many more geysers than those we saw in eruption there are in this remarkable basin, it is impossible to determine. We will be compelled reluctantly to leave it before it can be half explored. At least a thousand pipes rise to the plain, one or two hundred of which, to all appearances, are as likely to be geysers as any we have seen.

This entire country is seemingly under a constant and active internal pressure from volcanic forces, which seek relief through the numberless springs, jets, volcanoes and geysers exhibited on its surface, and which but for these vents might burst forth in one terrific eruption and form a volcano of vast dimensions. It is undoubtedly true that many of the objects we see are of recent formation, and that many of the extinguished craters recently ceased their condition of activity. They are constantly breaking forth, often

---

*James Bridger was famous for the marvelous stories he was accustomed to relate of his mountain life and experiences. He once told me that he had seen a river which flowed so rapidly over the smooth surface of a descending rock ledge in the bottom of the stream, that the water was "hot at the bottom." My experience in crossing the Firehole river that day, leads me to believe that Bridger had had, at some time, a similar experience. He well knew that heat and fire could be produced by friction. Like other mountain men, he had doubtless, many a time, produced a fire by friction; and he could not account for the existence of a hot rock in the bed of a cold stream, except upon the theory that the rapid flow of water over the smooth surface evolved the heat, by friction.

N. P. LANGFORD.

assuming new forms, and attesting to the active presence of volcanic force.

The water in some of the springs presents to the eye the colors of all the precious gems known to commerce. In one spring the hue is like that of an emerald, in another like that of the turquoise, another has the ultra-marine hue of the sapphire, another has the color of the topaz; and the suggestion has been made that the names of these jewels may very properly be given to many of these springs.

The packers with the pack train and several of our party broke camp at 9:30 this morning, a few of us remaining for an hour, hoping to have another view of an eruption of the "Giantess;" but in this we were disappointed, for it gave no sign of an eruption, save that the water, visible generally at a depth of about twenty feet, would rise suddenly eight or ten feet in the well, and as suddenly fall again.

We moved down the river on the east bank, part of the way through an open valley and part through fallen timber. At about eight miles we came upon an enormous spring of dark blue water, the largest we have seen. Mr. Hauser measured it, and says it is four hundred feet in diameter. The mineral solution has been deposited by the overflow on all sides for two hundred yards, the spring itself being thirty feet above the general level of the valley. Out near the center of the lake the water boils up a few feet, but without any especial violent action. The lake has no well-defined outlet, but overflows on many sides, the water flowing down the slopes of the incrusted mound about one-quarter of an inch deep. As we stood on the margin of this immense lake a small flock of ducks came sailing down as if to alight; but as they skimmed the water a few inches above the surface, they seemed to scent danger, and with rapid flapping of their wings, all except one rose into the air. This one, in his descent, had gained too great an impetus to check his progress, and came down into the water, and his frantic efforts to rise again were futile, and with one or two loud squawks of distress, which were responded to by his mates who had escaped, he was in a moment "a dead duck." We gave no name to this lake.*

About one hundred yards from the lake on the side towards the river, the incrustation breaks off perpendicularly, and another large lake is formed, the surface of which is about fifteen feet below the upper and larger lake. There are a few other springs near the river farther down the stream.

Jake Smith, for the first time on this trip, selected at this large lake a curious specimen of tufa. It was a circumstance so unusual that Hedges called our attention to it, but as Smith was riding along holding his treasure carefully in his hand, his horse stumbled, and he accidentally dropped his specimen, and with a remark which I will not here record, and which is at variance with his own Bible instruction, he denounced as worthless all the specimens of the party which he had seen, and inveighed against the folly of spending any time in gathering them.

From this point we passed down the valley close by the bank of the river. The valley on our right was very marshy, and we saw at a considerable distance one very large fountain of water spouting into the atmosphere to a considerable height, and many steam jets, but, owing to the swampy character of the ground, we did not visit them.*

When we left Helena on August 17th, we believed that twenty-five days would be the limit of time which would be consumed before our return; but to meet all exigencies

*This lake is now called "Hell's Half-acre;" and from the lower lake the "Excelsior" geyser has burst forth.

*The fountain and jets here referred to are those of the Lower Geyser Basin, and the larger column of water which we saw is undoubtedly the "Fountain" geyser, named by Dr. Hayden in 1871.

we laid in a thirty days' supply of provisions. We have now been absent thirty-four days, and as we cached some of our supply on Yellowstone lake for Mr. Everts' relief, we are now on short rations, but the fish we dried while camped on Yellowstone lake are doing good service.

While riding to-day alongside of Stickney and bemoaning the lack in our larder of many articles of food, such as sugar, coffee and tea, the supply of which has become exhausted, I asked him if he was fond of maple sugar, and would like a lump of it. He requested me not to tantalize him by mentioning the subject, whereupon I astonished him by producing a goodly sized cake which I had brought with me from Helena, and which for five weeks I had preserved untouched in my seamless sack. It was enjoyed by all who shared it, but Stickney was especially grateful for his division of the sweet morsel, and received it gratefully and gracefully, and seemingly without reluctance, at the same time remarking, "You are always doing something to make me laugh!" and added, "You always seem to have another card up your sleeve when an emergency arises." By this last figure of speech he delicately suggested to me the methods adopted by Jake Smith in playing poker.*

We have traveled to-day about eighteen miles, crossing just before the day closed a timbered ridge, and we are now camped at the junction of the Firehole river with a

---

*In the course of a recent correspondence with Mr. Stickney, I asked him if he recalled this incident. Under date of May 20, 1905, he wrote me from Sarasota, Florida: "The maple sugar incident had almost faded from my memory, but like a spark of fire smouldering under rubbish it needed but a breath to make it live, and I recall my reflections, after my astonishment, that you did so many quaint things, that it was quite in accordance with them that you should produce maple sugar in a sulphurous region."

N. P. LANGFORD.

stream coming into it from the east nearly as large as the Firehole, but to which we have given no name.*

Tuesday, September 20.—We broke camp at half past nine o'clock, traveling along the rocky edge of the river bank by the rapids, passing thence through a beautiful pine wood and over a long stretch of fallen timber, blackened by fire, for about four miles, when we again reached the river, which here bends in a westerly direction. Lieutenant Doane and I climbed to the top of one of the two prominent hills on our course, and had a fine view of the country for the distance of thirty miles.

Last night, and also this morning in camp, the entire party had a rather unusual discussion. The proposition was made by some member that we utilize the result of our exploration by taking up quarter sections of land at the most prominent points of interest, and a general discussion followed. One member of our party suggested that if there could be secured by pre-emption a good title to two or three quarter sections of land opposite the lower fall of the Yellowstone and extending down the river along the cañon, they would eventually become a source of great profit to the owners. Another member of the party thought that it would be more desirable to take up a quarter section of land at the Upper Geyser Basin, for the reason that that locality could be more easily reached by tourists and pleasure seekers. A third suggestion was that each member of the party pre-empt a claim, and in order that no one should have an advantage over the others, the whole should be thrown into a common pool for the benefit of the entire party.

Mr. Hedges then said that he did not approve of any of these plans—that there ought to be no private ownership

*This stream was afterwards named "Gibbon river."

of any portion of that region, but that the whole of it ought to be set apart as a great National Park, and that each one of us ought to make an effort to have this accomplished. His suggestion met with an instantaneous and favorable response from all—except one—of the members of our party, and each hour since the matter was first broached, our enthusiasm has increased. It has been the main theme of our conversation to-day as we journeyed. I lay awake half of last night thinking about it;—and if my wakefulness deprived my bed-fellow (Hedges) of any sleep, he has only himself and his disturbing National Park proposition to answer for it.

Our purpose to create a park can only be accomplished by untiring work and concerted action in a warfare against the incredulity and unbelief of our National legislators when our proposal shall be presented for their approval. Nevertheless, I believe we can win the battle.

I do not know of any portion of our country where a national park can be established furnishing to visitors more wonderful attractions than here. These wonders are so different from anything we have ever seen—they are so various, so extensive—that the feeling in my mind from the moment they began to appear until we left them has been one of intense surprise and of incredulity. Every day spent in surveying them has revealed to me some new beauty, and now that I have left them, I begin to feel a skepticism which clothes them in a memory clouded by doubt.

Wednesday, September 21.—We broke camp soon after 9 o'clock, traveling northwesterly down the stream, which at six miles entered a cañon extending ten miles in a very tortuous course, the stream gradually bending to the west. The sides of the cañon are steep, and a great many small lateral streams flow into it, forming cascades of remarkable beauty. There are also many springs gushing out from the sides of the cañon afar up.   Below the cañon we traveled over a high ridge for the distance of ten miles, and camped in a deep coulee, where we found good water and an abundance of wood and grass.   Mr. Hauser and Mr. Stickney all through the day were a few miles in advance of the rest of the party, and just below the mouth of the cañon they met two men who manifested some alarm at sight of them. They had a supply of provisions packed on riding saddles, and were walking beside their horses.   Mr. Hauser told them that they would meet a large party up the cañon, but we did not see them, and they evidently cached themselves as we went by.   The Upper Madison in this vicinity is said to be a rendezvous for horse thieves.   We have traveled about twenty-five miles to-day.

As the outcome of a general conversation to-night, I will leave the party to-morrow morning, and start for Virginia City, where I have a forlorn hope that some tidings may be had of Mr. Everts.   We think that Virginia City is not more than thirty miles distant; but, as we are not now on any trail leading to it, I shall have to take my chances of finding it.

Jake Smith to-day asked me if I expected that the readers of my diary would believe what I had written.   He said that he had kept no diary for the reason that our discoveries had been of such a novel character, that if he were to write an account of them he would not be believed by those who read his record, and he would be set down as a liar.   He said that he did not mind being called a liar by those who had known him well for many years, but he would not allow strangers that privilege.   This ambiguous remark indicates that Jake has more wit and philosophy than I have given him the credit of possessing.

Thursday, September 22, Virginia City.—With a small supply of needed creature comforts (lunch, etc.), I left the

party early this morning, uncertain as to the time which
would be required to take me to Virginia City.   About noon
I met a horseman who had left Virginia City this morning,
who directed me to the trail leading to the town.   He paused
long enough to let me scan a newspaper which he had, from
which I learned of the capitulation of the French at Sedan.
I asked him to hand the newspaper to General Washburn,
whose party he would meet in the Madison valley.   He said
that he would stop at the cabin of "Bannack George."

The distance from our morning camp to this place is much
farther than we thought, and it was 9 o'clock this evening
before I reached Virginia City.   Nothing has been heard of
Mr. Everts, and his friends are shocked at the intelligence
of his loss from our party.

Owing to the late hour of my arrival I have met but few
of my old acquaintances, but these are greatly interested in
the result of our explorations, and I have promised to remain here another day before starting for Helena, and give
them a further description of what I have seen.   I have enjoyed one good square meal.

Tuesday, September 27, Helena.—I reached Helena last
night.   The intelligence of my arrival in Virginia City, and
of the loss of Mr. Everts from our party, had been tele-
graphed to Helena from Virginia City, and on my arrival
I was besieged by many of the friends of Mr. Everts for information concerning the manner in which he became separated from our party.   I have spent the larger part of this
day in describing the many wonders which we found on our
trip, and I shall be most glad to have a few days' rest and
put on some of my lost flesh.   At the outset of this journey
I tipped the beam of the scales at a little over one hundred
and ninety (190) pounds, and to-day I weigh but one hundred and fifty-five (155) pounds, a loss of thirty-five (35)
pounds.   One of my friends says that I may consider myself

fortunate in bringing back to civilization as much of my body as I did. I have already received several invitations from householders to meet their families and friends at their homes, and tell them of our trip, but the present dilapidated condition of my toilet renders it necessary for me to decline their hospitalities until some future period. My first duty to myself and my fellow citizens is to seek a tailor and replenish my wardrobe. Jake Smith is the only one of our party who has returned with a garment fit to wear in the society of ladies.

My narrations to-day have excited great wonder, and I cannot resist the conviction that many of my auditors believe that I have "drawn a long bow" in my descriptions. I am perfectly free to acknowledge that this does not surprise me. It seems a most natural thing for them to do so; for, in the midst of my narrations, I find myself almost as ready to doubt the reality of the scenes I have attempted to describe as the most skeptical of my listeners. They pass along my memory like the faintly defined outlines of a dream. And when I dwell upon their strange peculiarities, their vastness, their variety, and the distinctive features of novelty which mark them all, so entirely out of the range of all objects that compose the natural scenery and wonders of this continent, I who have seen them can scarcely realize that in those far-off recesses of the mountains they have existed so long in impenetrable seclusion, and that hereafter they will stand foremost among the natural attractions of the world. Astonishment and wonder become so firmly impressed upon the mind in the presence of these objects, that belief stands appalled, and incredulity is dumb. You can see Niagara, comprehend its beauties, and carry from it a memory ever ready to summon before you all its grandeur. You can stand in the valley of the Yosemite, and look up its mile of vertical granite, and distinctly recall its minutest feature; but amid the cañon and falls, the boiling springs and sulphur mountain, and, above all, the mud volcano and the geysers of the Yellowstone, your memory becomes filled and clogged with objects new in experience, wonderful in extent, and possessing unlimited grandeur and beauty. It is a new phase in the natural world; a fresh exhibition of the handiwork of the Great Architect; and, while you see and wonder, you seem to need an additional sense, fully to comprehend and believe.

APPENDIX.

It is much to be regretted that our expedition was not accompanied by an expert photographer; but at the time of our departure from Helena, no one skilled in the art could be found with whom the hazards of the journey did not outweigh any seeming advantage or compensation which the undertaking promised.

The accompanying sketches of the two falls of the Yellowstone, and of the cones of the Grand and Castle geysers, were made by Walter Trumbull and Private Moore. They are the very first ever made of these objects. Through an inadvertence in the preparation of the electroyped plates for the printer, they did not appear in their proper places in this diary. Major Hiram M. Chittenden, in his volume "The Yellowstone Park," says of the two sketches made by Private Moore: "His quaint sketches of the falls forcibly remind one of the original picture of Niagara, made by Father Hennepin, in 1697."

GIANT GEYSER CONE.
ORIGINAL SKETCH.

CASTLE GEYSER CONE.
ORIGINAL SKETCH.

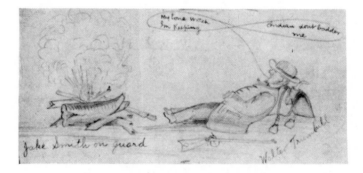

DOING GUARD DUTY.

ORIGINAL SKETCH.

Upper Fall Yellowstone
115 ft.

Moore.

UPPER FALL OF THE YELLOWSTONE.

ORIGINAL SKETCH.

LOWER FALL OF THE YELLOWSTONE.

ORIGINAL SKETCH.

INDEX